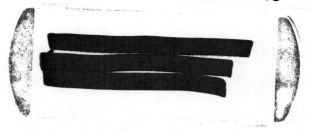

IN LOVE AND IN DANGER

IN
LOVE
AND
IN
DANGER

A Teen's Guide to Breaking
Free of Abusive Relationships

BARRIE LEVY

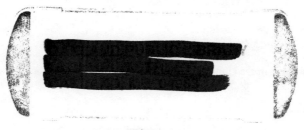

SEAL PRESS

Published by Seal Press
An Imprint of Avalon Group, Inc.
1400 65th Street, Suite 250
AVALON Emeryville, CA 94608
publishing group incorporated

Book design by Clare Conrad
Cover design by Joe Kaftan

Library of Congress Cataloging-in-Publication Data

Levy, Barrie
    In love and in danger : a teen's guide to breaking free of abusive
relationships / Barrie Levy.
    Summary: Describes the experiences of teens who have had abusive dating
relationships and gives advice on how to end the cycle of abuse and forge
healthy and loving, violence-free relationships.
    1. Dating violence—United States—Juvenile literature. 2. Dating violence—
United States—Prevention—Juvenile literature. 3. Teenage girls—United
States—Abuse of—Juvenile literature.
    [1. Dating Violence.]   I. Title.
HQ801.83.L48   1992
306.73'0835—dc20   92-41914
ISBN 1-58005-002-6

Printed in the United States of America by Sheridan Books
10 9 8 7 6 5 4 3

Distributed to the trade by Publisher's Group West
In Canada: Publisher's Group West Canada, Toronto, Ontario
In Australia: Bookwise International, Wingfield, South Australia
In the United Kingdom, Europe and South Africa: Hi Marketing, London
In Asia and the Middle East: Michelle Morrow Curreri, Beverly, MA

Acknowledgments

Thank you to the people of all ages who, dedicated to helping teens have violence-free relationships, have helped make this book possible. Once again, it has been a pleasure to work with Faith Conlon at Seal Press. Linda Fischer and others at Project PAVE in Denver encouraged young men to share their experiences as abusers. Ruth Beaglehole at the Business Industry School in Los Angeles involved her students in reviewing the manuscript, and provided priceless feedback at crucial stages in writing this book. Linda's and Ruth's enthusiasm and dedication to youth are inspirational.

Adaliz, Deborah and Terrie spent hours telling their stories and reliving their nightmares to prevent other girls and parents from having to go through the kinds of violence they experienced.

Coralyn Mills from the City of Seattle's Prosecutor's Office; Claudia Cuevas from California State University at Northridge; Ken Greene and Cathy Chadwick, who worked for years with children in battered women's shelters; and Denise Gamache, now with WHISPER, and formerly with the Minnesota Coalition for Battered Women, interviewed young women whose words appear on these pages. Margaret Anderson, Salina Stone, Jan Jenson, Meybel Guzman, Elizabeth, Bonnie Zimmer and Felicia—who wrote their stories in *Dating Violence: Young Women in Danger*—contributed again to educating young women and men about the realities of dating violence. Ann G. contributed her story as well.

Sheila Kuehl provided legal information, and Ginny

NiCarthy provided material for the section on addictive love—both from their contributions to *Dating Violence: Young Women in Danger.*

I have a wonderful cheering squad: I am indebted to my daughter, Johanna, for her review and suggestions about the manuscript, and to Linda Garnets, for brainstorming, support and inspiration.

Contents

IN LOVE AND IN DANGER

■ Introduction

This book is for teenagers who have questions about abusive dating relationships. Are you in a relationship with someone you love who is hurting you? Were you in one in the past? Do you have a friend or family member who is a teenager and is being hit? Verbally abused? Sexually abused? Do you treat someone you love abusively?

If you answered yes, you are not alone. There are many other young women and men who are having the same or similar problems. And there are people who can help you deal with it so you don't have to feel so alone.

This book will help you to understand what is happening to you, and if what is happening in your relationship is "abuse." It will help you decide what you can do about it.

This book is for teens to share with friends, parents, other family members, teachers, counselors and others.

In the first section, you will read stories told by two girls and a mother about their experiences with dating violence. The sections following the stories give you general information about dating violence. They end with a summary of the information in that section and an "Exercise" page for your thoughts and feelings.

Hopefully, this book will leave you feeling encouraged and empowered to confront a very difficult teenage problem.

1 *Speaking Out*

■*Deborah: "It Was Love at First Sight"*

It was love at first sight. It was at my first job, and Larry was Mr. Personality. When he started paying attention to me, I was so excited. I was fifteen. He was seventeen, older than me and already driving. He was totally romantic. He'd take me out to really nice dinners. We'd dress up and go to nice places. He'd bring me flowers and write me poetry and love letters. It was incredibly intense.

He was the first guy I ever dated. It was great to have a boyfriend. My friends seemed to respect me more now that I had a boyfriend, and they thought he was a great guy. My family liked him. He was a nice Jewish boy, from a nice family. He could be so "tough." He'd want to kick anyone's ass who looked at me. I was excited, and flattered.

It was wonderful having a boyfriend who wanted to spend all of our time together. I felt at home with him, warm, connected. He'd help me with my school work. We'd just want to stay home and be together. Those were good times. I believed I could never be with another human being and feel so totally connected. No one else mattered.

The stuff that happened to other girls never happened to me, like waiting and the guy doesn't call. Larry was so passionate. He always wanted me, and he always wanted all of my time. After the first date, well, he just assumed we were together: "When are you going to see me tomorrow...?"

But pretty soon other things began to happen too. If we

went out for dinner with my family, as soon as we were where they couldn't hear us, he'd fight with me about them. He'd say, "Your dad is stupid; he said this or that," or other critical things. It got to be easier not to be with them, to avoid fights, so he wouldn't find fault with them.

He started talking shit about my friends. He never said, "You can't see your friends." He just ridiculed them, said mean things about them, and fought with me about them so it seemed it was only acceptable to spend time with his friends.

He was jealous of everyone, and started treating me like his possession. At first it was not that obvious. He'd ridicule guys I had been friends with for a long time before I met him. Then he made it clear it was a "rule": I couldn't talk to guys or maintain my friendships with them. If he saw me talking to a guy, he'd ask suspiciously, "Why are you talking to that guy? What did you say to him?" He'd say, "I really love you, and I'm all you need." If any guy smiled at me when we were out, he'd say, "That son of a bitch! He really wants you." He'd accuse me of provoking it. He was twisted. He thought about sex with everyone.

One day he convinced me that my closest girlfriend was after him. He'd say that a lot, when we went places, that girls were looking at him, or that a girlfriend of mine was going after him. This time, he convinced me that we had to go over to my girlfriend's house to confront her. So we went over there and ridiculed her, told her off. I have regretted doing that forever.

If something happened to upset him, he'd scream, yell at me in front of his friends or his family. When I was seventeen, we went to Las Vegas with my family. One day he wanted to wear a shirt of mine. I said no, he'd stretch it out. In front of my family, he yelled at me that I was selfish, a lousy person, worthless. He verbally attacked me—over a shirt! Then he bought me flowers and told me he got mad at me because he loved me. My parents were disappointed. They didn't like for me to go out with him after that.

One and a half years after meeting Larry, I got sick. It was diagnosed as Hodgkin's Disease. It was a dark year. Larry was there, my only friend. After the treatments for cancer, I got better, and he said that I allowed this to happen to myself because I'm not positive, because I'm weak, inferior. But I always thought of how he stayed with me, going through that terrible year with me. And I'd always remember how he loved me so much. So even when it got bad being with him, I'd think of that, and feel like I couldn't live without him, my only friend.

He didn't hit me. But I always thought he would, if I made him mad. The stuff he did was mind-twisting. Sometimes I thought it would be better if he hit me. I'd think, "If he gave me a black eye, I'd know what was wrong." But I was so confused. He'd search my purse and go through my things, finding things so he could accuse me of seeing someone or doing something wrong. If I brought up a subject to talk about or if I disagreed with him when we were with friends, he'd ridicule me publicly. I walked on eggshells. I never talked about anything important with him and other people.

He constantly told me I looked ugly, heavy, like an old lady. He made me cut my hair short, though I loved it long. He watched what I ate, and put me on a workout program. No matter how much or how well I did he criticized me for doing badly. I was always too fat or too weak. For example, when I did forty-seven pushups, and couldn't get to fifty, he'd make me start over, and tell me I was too weak.

Then, every time, after he got mad, he'd turn around and get me gifts and say, "I love you." I'd say, "He wouldn't hurt me; he loves me. I must be crazy."

A while after he got a new car, I accidentally dropped my compact and spilled powder in the car. He got so mad, he opened the car door and tried to push me out on the freeway. One time, I borrowed his car when mine was being repaired. I carefully parked it in the driveway of my friend's house so nothing could happen to it. While I was there, the next-door neighbors put on their sprinklers and got the car wet. I was so scared, I was shaking. When I brought his car back to him, it had water spots. "You idiot! You moron!" he yelled at me, in my face, spitting at me, for what felt like forever. His family was there, watching. They didn't say anything. I saw darkness, as if I were passing out.

After he'd scream and yell at me about something that made him mad, and he'd call me an idiot, or a fucking bitch, then he'd want to make love. He'd always say, "If you didn't say that or act that way, I wouldn't get mad." He'd say he got so mad because he loved me. He said I was lucky to have him, no other guy would want me or look at me.

I couldn't make any decisions, even easy ones, like if I wanted soup or salad. I'd look at him, and ask, "What do I want?" If I wanted what he wanted it was okay. I was only comfortable if he made all the decisions. Then I knew I was okay, safe. I'd only be comfortable with his friends and his family, doing his things. I was too uncomfortable around my friends or my family. I was always looking at him to see if I was okay, always afraid to displease him, to make him mad, and never sure if I was okay or doing something wrong.

I still feel ashamed to talk about sex. I had sex with him when I didn't want to. He'd tell me how other women did it, and what other women like. He often wanted me to have sex with another woman and with him, together. I avoided it. He wanted sex all the time, and he told me something was wrong with me because I didn't want sex enough.

The first time we ever had sex, it was beautiful. It was on graduation night, on the beach. I trusted him. It was romantic, perfect. I wanted to have sex with him, to be close to him. That first night is painted clearly in my mind. He knew what to do, and I was totally inexperienced. It didn't hurt, like other girls say happens the first time. It was like I was being taken care of in a comforting way.

We were always sneaking somewhere to make love or to spend time together. We couldn't be apart. I believed two people became one, which I don't feel now, but then I had this sense of oneness. I felt good about myself because I had this wonderful man. My friends thought he was great because he was so romantic. He'd bring balloons or flowers to me at school. No matter how bad it got, there were always these wonderful moments. I felt protected, under his wings —a safe place at times. Then it became a frightening place at times.

After the beginning, sex turned bad. It hurt. He forced me to do it in positions that were painful. He made me do things that felt humiliating, like when he made me masturbate in front of him. I began to hate it. All I wanted was "spoons," to cuddle. He told me men have to have sex; if they don't ejaculate often, they get in a bad mood. He said that was the reason for his rage and anger. Later I felt stupid when I found out this wasn't true.

I never said no, but I didn't want it. I'd just die. I'd mentally be in a dark place in a corner of the room watching. I'd think, "Take my body; do what you want. But you can't take me completely." I know now I was surviving. But then I thought I was crazy...and he'd tell me I was crazy. I started to believe something was wrong with me. Now I think maybe he raped me. I was so afraid to say no to him. I had no voice.

I tried to kill myself in different ways. Once I stepped on

the gas in an alley, took off my safety belt, and started to drive into a wall. But something stopped me.

I finally had it because he was so controlling. I wanted to have fun, to have freedom, the way my friends did. So I broke up with him. Larry kept calling. He was frantic, and pressuring me to get back together. I didn't want to see him. My parents wanted me to get away from him, so they arranged for me to go to Israel for a few months. The first week after we broke up, it hurt, but it got better and better. When I got back from Israel, I started dating another guy. I was seeing all my friends, and I was having fun. It was not the romance and fine restaurants. It was the normal kid stuff, like roller skating and hanging out. I could be myself. People listened to me when I talked. I went to college. I felt good.

But then the guy I was dating broke up with me, when he went away to a different college, to "do his thing." I couldn't handle it. Larry was still calling me. He was security. I knew he would be there, that he still loved me. I had grown my hair long. He said, "My god, you got heavy!" I was a size seven at the time. I thought, "Oh, god, I got fat again. I look like an old lady." He talked about his sexual escapades. I thought, "Thank goodness I have him again; I need him."

A year later, we got married. Larry's abuse escalated on our honeymoon. After we were married, it wasn't romantic. Suddenly, he wanted me to do everything for him. I went to school and had a full-time job, and did everything to take care of the house. If I ever did anything for myself, he'd punish me by making me do the laundry or something when I got home. He wanted complete control over me, our money, our home, everything. He forced me to quit college. He controlled me even at my jobs. He started hitting me.

I didn't think I could live on my own, or do anything

without Larry. I didn't have the confidence to leave home on my own. When we got married, I thought it was the way out of my parents' house, the way to be independent. Was I wrong! It was worse! I was *more* restricted by Larry than I ever was by my parents!

Before I left him, Larry was shoving me, spitting at me, lifting me up and shaking me. I was totally intimidated by him. I'd pray he'd die. I thought, "I can't ever leave him." I wanted to die, but I thought if he'd die, I'd be free.

But, with my brother's help, I went to see a therapist, and I gradually got my strength back, and I finally left Larry for good.

I am married now to a man who is thoughtful, gentle, comfortable, warm and safe. We have passion and friendship. We don't have the intense highs and lows that I had with Larry. We make decisions together, and he encourages me to do things that are important to me. We are good for each other.

Only recently I realized that what I experienced with Larry was emotional abuse. I didn't know it was wrong. We had such an incredible bond to each other, it was hard to break away. But Larry really hurt me. Now that I'm myself again, I know that even if I never have that intense bond again, I will never be treated badly like that again.

■ *Adaliz Rodriguez: "I Thought Things Would Change"*

I was twelve years old when I met Richard. I had lots of friends, but I never had a boyfriend before then. Richard was very popular. He was quiet, a sweetheart. I was madly in love with him. (Now I look back, and I realize it was junior high school—and the excitement of my first boyfriend.) My parents didn't allow me to see him because I was too young. So I told them I stopped seeing him, but I didn't. I started hiding things from them.

Richard and I started acting really serious, as if we were older. He started getting possessive. I wanted to enroll in the Drill Team, but he said no, those girls were all sluts. He made me feel guilty, so I didn't enroll. That was the beginning of him telling me what to do, and making me feel guilty and bad about everything.

I remember the first time he hit me. I met him at the corner to walk to school. I had on a light blouse with a slip under it. He thought you could see through it. I told him if my mother let me leave the house with it on, there was nothing wrong with it. He got mad and called me a bitch. He socked me in the face and knocked me down. I couldn't go home. What was I gonna tell my mom? So, crying, I went to school with Richard, and when we got there I changed into my gym clothes and wore those all day. I never wore that blouse again because I was afraid of him.

From that day on he told me how to dress and who to talk to. If I did something "wrong" (which means that made him jealous), I would fix it and do what he asked me to. I didn't want to make him mad. I think now, "If I could have put my foot down then, would he have stopped?" Maybe. A lot of girls are like me, and do what I did. They're scared and don't want to lose the guy.

Our problem was always his jealousy. I wasn't going out

with anyone, but he always thought I was looking at someone, or he thought my clothes were too tight, or that I was messing up or that I walked too sexy. How, at the age of thirteen, could he even think of those things?

What hurt me the most were his mean words. I wasn't used to the kind of names he called me. My parents never allowed that kind of language. I cried a lot. I walked looking down. I'd ditch school a lot, and, although I made sure I passed, I was falling behind. I was miserable. I'd tell him he was hurting me verbally. I'd try to break up with him, then he'd cry and say, "I'm sorry, don't leave me. I'll stop hitting you." I'd believe him, because I didn't want to leave him; I wanted him to change.

When I was in eighth grade, Richard was a grade ahead of me, and we were in separate schools. He would ditch school so he could walk me to school and pick me up. He had to make sure I wasn't doing anything. He'd find out from his friends if I was talking to someone, and we'd get in a big argument. He'd call me disgusting names, and make me cry. He'd hit me, push me, sock me in the stomach and in the head. He was smart. He knew not to leave me with bruises that showed.

He told me about problems his parents had. He used to jump on his father to stop him from hitting his mother. He said he'd never hit me like his father did. Then when he hit me, he'd say he didn't mean to, and turn it around so that it was my fault: "If you just didn't do those things, I wouldn't hit you." In other words, I shouldn't get him mad, or provoke him to hit me.

After a while, my parents found out I was still seeing him. My friends would tell their mothers, who would tell my mom. My sister would also tell my mom. She would question me, but I would say no. I was close to my father, and he tried to talk to me. My parents started taking me to

school. They did everything they could to stop me from seeing him. The more they kept me away from him, the more I
wanted to be with him. I ask myself now, why did I let that
go on?

When I went into ninth grade, I went to the same school
as Richard. My parents hunted everywhere for a different
school for me. The other schools wouldn't allow the trans-
fer. I was happy—I wanted to be in the same school as him.

As our relationship continued, and after we started having sex, the violence was worse and worse. He didn't like
anything I wore or did. His power to control me made him
feel good. He was always pushing me to have sex. One time,
we were already in school, and he wanted me to ditch because he wanted to have sex. He wanted to go to his house
because his parents weren't home. I said no, I didn't want
to. He dragged me by the hair, socking me. We were near a
field at school where students and a teacher were planting a
garden. The teacher called the narcs [school police]. They
handcuffed and arrested him. I wanted to go back to school,
but they made me go with them, and they called my parents.
My dad came to school, and told them to press charges. My
dad convinced the principal to get the school near where he
works to admit me there. The school permitted it because of
the situation, on the condition that I would do good work in
school.

Now my parents knew about the abuse. So my dad
would take me and pick me up every day. I couldn't go
anywhere. I couldn't make calls. My parents answered the
phone, and wouldn't let me talk to Richard if he called. I
thought my dad was a mean person. Now I realize that he
didn't want it to come out like it did. He didn't want me to
be hurt.

All I wanted was to be with Richard. So I ran away from
home to be with him, and lived with him at his aunt and un-

cle's house for one and a half months. But his jealousy, mean talk and hitting got worse. I thought being with him would make me happy, but I was miserable. After one incident when he accused me of "fucking" his uncle, I couldn't take it anymore, and I went home to my parents'.

But I continued to see him, even though I didn't want to live with him (I was fourteen). By the time I went home, I was pregnant. I hid it for six months. I thought my parents were going to kick me out or something. They are very religious, Jehovah's Witnesses. We never talked about abortion or adoption. I kept the baby. But even then they didn't allow me to see Richard.

Richard beat me worse when I was pregnant. He always aimed for my stomach and the back of my head. It was always because he thought I was looking at a guy, or some guy looked at me. Two weeks before my daughter was due, I went with my sister to see her boyfriend. Richard was there. Right away, he wanted to have sex. I told him no because I didn't feel good, and all those people were there. He got mad, and pushed me so that I fell straight back. I had so much pain I screamed. My sister was so angry. Richard said he was sorry, he was under so much stress because he couldn't see me.

The next day I had the baby. He came to see me that day and while he was there the doctor came in to check me. He got mad and yelled, "He had to touch you?" I said, "He's a doctor!"

The second time I was pregnant, I also had the baby early because he beat me. We got married while I was pregnant with our second daughter, when I was sixteen. We lived with my parents. I continued in high school—in eleventh grade. I wanted to graduate with my class.

Richard went to college to study computers and worked at night. We didn't see each other that much, and when we did, we fought a lot. Living with my parents was full of stress. Many times I left the house because I got fed up with him hitting me.

When I was around his mother, she would get mad at me: I shouldn't provoke her son to hit me. Everything was my fault. She didn't like my parents. Richard's mom used to say to my mom, "Why are you taking care of your daughter; she's not a virgin any more." She would tell my mom I'm a slut. My mom had more class than to say anything. My father would talk to Richard, open the Bible, and say, this is the way to treat your wife. Sometimes I wished he would beat Richard up and tell him to stop beating me. Now I'm glad my dad's not that kind of man.

I thought when we got married things would change, and he would stop beating me. I thought, "God, why should he hit me anymore? He can see me all the time. Everything I do, he'll see. He'll trust me." But he got worse. I was his now; he thought he owned me. Over the next four years, the violence got worse.

When we were in church, he pinched me and called me "Bitch!" when men were around. He hit me whenever he thought another man looked at me. He attacked my womanhood, for example, he often pinched me and socked me on my breasts, and kicked me between my legs. He dragged me down the steps by my hair. He slammed my hand in the front door. He kicked me with steel-toed boots after knocking me on the ground.

Several times when he hit me I called the cops. My parents now knew because they could hear him socking me. I'd deny it, and say I fell. My daughters would cry when they saw him hitting me. Sometimes they cried even when someone was playing, or my sister tickled me.

I tried everything. I'd throw clothes away he didn't like. I never even thought of having an affair. I was a good wife.

He never had to ask me to wash his clothes or to take care of the girls or cook meals. Everything was always done. I was so careful to never give him a reason to get mad and beat me.

Two years ago, after our son was born, things got worse again. Richard socked me in the face and broke my nose—and something snapped inside me. I didn't care anymore. I didn't plan to stop loving him. But something clicked, and I said, "I am not gonna go through this no more and that's it." I realized that this guy's not going to stop at anything. I left Richard.

He wouldn't face the fact that I left him because of the violence. He was sure I left him for another man. Richard still wants to get back together. He says he's changed. He has promised so many times he'd never hit me again, I don't believe him. Right now, it scares me to think of being with another man. It took me a lot of courage to get up and leave him. Since we separated, I am still trying to understand why he did that to me. I am twenty-one, and I have a lot I want to do with my life. I am stronger now, and I want to talk to other girls like me, so they won't stay with a boyfriend who abuses them like Richard abused me.

• Postscript: An Excuse to Blow Up
Richard was interviewed for a story on teen dating violence that appeared in the *L.A. Times* on October 13, 1991. The following are excerpts from that story.

"We were at school," says Richard, a compact young man. "I don't know what it was, but I pushed her and I hit her very hard. The [school police officers] seen us and it opened my eyes. What am I doing? They handcuffed me, which I deserved, and slammed me against a table. I was scared of myself and of what I was growing up to be. I was thirteen."

But the incident did not end the violence. No charges were filed because of his age, the couple stayed together despite their parents' protests, and Richard continued to abuse Adaliz.

"She was the only person who was there," Richard says. "And when you care about somebody, you take it out on them. I couldn't do it on my mom and dad. They would hit me. So I would make up an excuse to blow up—'Why are you wearing that? What are you doing?'"

Richard fits a pattern. He became vigilant and controlling and jealous of anything his girlfriend might do that threatened him and his dependence on her.

"I got to the point where I wouldn't let her wear this or that," he says. "I didn't like her to wear white because people could see through it. I would call her a whore. . . . I don't know what it was. Maybe I was insecure and she is a very attractive girl."

Richard says that when he was seven, he forced himself, though terrified, out of his bedroom to push his father, who was beating his mother.

Yet when Adaliz would appear at Richard's house with bruises, his mother would ask her, "What did you do to provoke him?"

A year and a half ago, after he broke her nose, she left him. Richard claims the final episode has changed him, too. "That is when I opened my eyes," he says. "I never broke anything before."

Now, he says, he wants her back and swears he would never hit her.

■ *Terrie Walsh: "She Was a Prisoner"*

I met Bobbie's new boyfriend Josh for the first time at her sixteenth birthday party. He was nineteen, and he came with a group of girls and boys who were Bobbie's new friends. They were different from her old friends. She didn't tell me much about them, but I heard their names more and more during the next few months, and I saw less and less of her old friends.

Bobbie was a straight A student. She won a journalism award when she was a junior in high school. She was a talented ice skater, and attended acting classes twice a week at a well-known theater group. By the time she was fourteen, she was already beautiful. She always took great pride in her appearance, putting on makeup before going to school every day, and dressing carefully. She was very outgoing and funny, always laughing and joking. She was loving and eager to please. She got along well with everyone, and never gave us any reason to worry about her. That was before she met Josh.

At first, when Josh came to the house, he dressed nicely and he was polite. I had just had a baby, and he was friendly, and proposed that we all do things together.

My husband and I began to become uncomfortable about Bobbie's relationship with Josh because he was so different from her. For example, he was not interested in school, and he wasn't as active as she was. We decided to "see how it goes." We were afraid that if we pressured her or told her what to do, she would do the opposite. We figured she would get tired of him.

Then Josh started coming around looking awful. He'd come over barefoot, with no shirt and filthy hair, with an open beer can in his hand. He would go right to Bobbie's bedroom and shut the door.

I would tell her not to shut the door, and that Josh couldn't come over looking the way he did. He was disrespectful. Bobbie would get upset. She started getting critical of everything going on in the family. Her manner became completely different. When I asked her about her old friends, there was always a problem with *them*: This one was too busy, that one had a new boyfriend she didn't like. Her friends stopped calling or coming around.

I found out she was skipping school when I started getting calls from the school counselor. The first time, I was shocked to find out she hadn't been in school for a whole week, and that she had given the school a note with my forged signature. I'd ask her about it, and she'd overreact, sobbing and denying it. I realized later that she was hanging out with Josh rather than going to school.

Her appearance started changing. She stopped wearing makeup. She went out with dirty hair and in sweats and torn sneakers. She started losing weight. She was already small, and during that year she went from 118 to 90 pounds. She had colds and sore throats constantly.

I thought she was trying to get attention because she was jealous of the baby. I really didn't see all of these changes as signs that Josh was hurting her, and that they were using drugs. I finally realized he was hurting her when I got a call one day from Josh's mother. She asked me, "Do you know where Bobbie is?" She told me that Josh had torn apart her house with lead pipes and, with a gun, had taken Bobbie in her car and disappeared. His mother had called the police, and they had an all points bulletin out. I was terrified. An hour later, I got a call from Bobbie, from a 7-11 thirty miles away, saying, "Come get me!" My husband went to get her. The side of her car was bashed in. Bobbie said, "We had a fight, and Josh drove his truck into the side of the car."

Josh was picked up by the police a few days later, and

was jailed for a week. Bobbie was at home, falling apart. When he got out of jail, he showed up at our house at one o'clock in the morning. He wanted money from Bobbie so he could leave town. I wouldn't let Bobbie leave the house. She gave him some money, and he left.

My husband and I decided the next day to send her away to boarding school. She cried, relieved. She was glad he was gone, and glad she had parents who could do this for her. We told the school to call us if this guy ever came around.

Four months later, we got a call from the school. Bobbie had left with Josh. She called us from a resort one hundred miles from here, and told us in a mean and nasty way that was not like her that she wasn't going back to school. I got in my car and found her and took her back to school. This happened four or five times, until we enrolled her in public school and she returned home because she just wouldn't go to the boarding school.

The problems started again, and it was clear to us that she was so involved with Josh and with drugs that she defied whatever we did to stop it. People started coming around to our house at one or two o'clock in the morning looking for drugs, and finally we told her, "You can't do drugs here." When she left, I thought she'd be back in a couple of days. She was gone for a year. She called a few days later and told me where she was living with Josh. She had dropped out of school.

During that year, I called the police many times, I went to get Bobbie and brought her home many times, and I kept trying to get her the help she needed to get off drugs. Each time, Josh would come to get her, and she would go back with him.

But Bobbie and I did stay in touch. I did everything I could to keep her in our family. I kept hoping that her ties to her family would be strong enough to help her get through all this, and come home.

On Mother's Day, I picked her up to bring her home for dinner. One eye was black and blue, her nose was swollen and had been bleeding and she had a swollen lip. She said she had been in a fight with a girl. I didn't believe her, but she stuck to her story. Finally I said, "If you're getting hurt, I want you to get medical care. I'll pay for it. Just get yourself to a good place to get the care you need."

A short time later, I got a call late at night from the hospital emergency room. She had a split lip, swollen eyes and was dehydrated from drugs. The nurse said that her boyfriend had dropped her off, and she was crying for him. "I want Josh." She said, "I told him to take me here because you said I should, but he was mad. Please call him. I have to be with him. I can't leave him!" I took her home, but she disappeared again.

I became obssessed about her. All I thought about was if she'd be alive the next day. I'd have to call her at six o'clock in the morning to see if she was alive.

Sometimes when I called her she wasn't there. Once, she wasn't there for three or four days, so I went over to look around. An older woman rented a house in back of theirs. I asked her if she had seen Bobbie. She asked me in to sit down. "Are you a Christian woman?" she asked. "All you can do is pray for her. Josh took her away in his truck. He has guns." I asked her to call me when Bobbie came back, or whenever Bobbie was in trouble. She was frightened, but finally she agreed.

That morning at one o'clock in the morning she called. Bobbie's back, and it's quiet. After that, she called me many times.

Bobbie's life with Josh was a nightmare. He was intensely jealous. He wouldn't let her see her friends or her family. He wouldn't let her come over for Sunday dinners. She would say she couldn't come unless he could come too.

She would visit sometimes when he would drop her off for an hour and then come back and pick her up. He'd wait outside in his truck. Or she would call me when he wasn't home, and ask me to help her with something, or say, "I want to see you, but I only have an hour." Any place we went, she'd have to rush to get back when he said or when he got home.

On her seventeenth birthday, I took her out for lunch, and we met at a restaurant. He dropped her off, she came in, rushed, and said, "Let's eat fast, because he's coming at one-thirty." She'd be so frightened, and worried about not doing what he said. When we'd go shopping for clothes, she restricted herself and wouldn't buy things she liked. She could never wear a bikini, only a one-piece bathing suit. "He'd never let me wear that," she'd say in fear.

He wouldn't let her have things she needed or money to buy them. She called once because she needed Tampax, and he wouldn't let her go out, or give her money to buy some. A couple of times when I saw her she hadn't eaten in a few days.

Josh controlled everything. He gave her things to his friends. She wasn't allowed to call me. She warned me not to call her, saying she'd call me when he was gone. She was a prisoner.

He'd burn her clothes—because he'd get mad at how she looked, or because I got them for her. He slit a leather jacket I got her for her birthday with his knife.

If he got mad at her, he beat her, knocked her out, or threw her out. Once the old woman called me because Bobbie was outside crying hysterically in a rain storm. It was pouring outside. He had beaten her and thrown her outside and locked her out. She was drenched and cold and he wouldn't let her back in the house.

Bobbie was always trying to save Josh. "He doesn't have a family," she'd say. Or, "He never had Christmas." Or, "He never had books." She believed that if only she could do enough for him, or give him all the things *she* had, he'd change—because he'd love it so much, he'd become more like her.

Sometimes she wouldn't see me because she couldn't stand for me to see her the way she was, beaten, a prisoner. She told me later that those days when I couldn't find her, she was staying away from me. "I wanted to come home, but I didn't want my mom to see me like that." She was also afraid for us. Josh threatened to hurt the baby, or to do something violent to all of us. So she stayed away to keep him away from her family.

I kept trying to get her away from him. I'd get her into drug treatment programs, and she'd stay for a few days. Then Josh would come to get her and she'd leave with him. We spent so much money trying to get her help. It ripped our family apart. I was always afraid she was going to die.

One day I was about to leave to meet her for lunch, and I got a call from the woman in the back house. "Come now!" she said. "I don't know if she's dead or alive! There was a huge fight. She's lying on the front lawn." I raced over.

Bobbie was unconscious on the grass. Her stuff was thrown out there—her clothes, her radio. I shook her and woke her up. The side of her head was one huge bruise. I took her to the emergency room. After kicking her all over, Josh had held a plant in a clay pot over her head as she lay on the ground, and he dropped it. She rolled away in time so that it caught the side of her head. If it had hit her where he aimed it, she would have been killed. The police came; she filed charges. When they took photographs of her at the police station, she was bruised everywhere—her legs, her back, everywhere.

She was in the hospital for a few days, then Bobbie said she was ready. I took her to my sister's in Massachusetts, 3,000 miles away. She stayed a month, and when she came home, she was herself again. She had her old friends over to the house. She got into counseling, and she attended a support group for battered women. She enrolled in the community college.

One day, Josh met her in the parking lot at school after her class. She came home from school, and went out that night in her old sweats. I knew Josh was back. She stayed out all night. She called the next morning. "Mom, come get me. I left while he was sleeping. I'm never going back. I just had to see what it was like, to know for sure that I'm never going back to that." I was furious. I told her she had to get out of town, that he'd always find her. Twenty-four hours later, the day before her eighteenth birthday, I took her to the airport, and she went to live with my sister in Massachusetts.

She worked for a while, then decided to go to college. She started dating a boy who was a little younger than she was, and he invited her to his high school prom. They went to football games, and she did all of the things she had missed out on in high school.

Bobbie went to school in Massachusetts for three years. Josh has shown up a couple of times. My husband and I have called the police, and, the last time, when Josh apologized to us for all of the trouble he has put us through, we told him that if that meant anything he would never come here again. Bobbie said to me recently, "I hope that some day I won't be scared of Josh!" She said, "The hook of violence is so intense. I'll never love anyone the way I loved him. And it was so overwhelming, I can't talk about it without crying."

2 *Facts About Dating Violence*

Now that you just finished reading the stories told by Adaliz, by Deborah and by Terrie at the beginning of this book, you may be having all kinds of intense feelings. Did you see yourself, or your friend, or someone you care about in these stories? Did you realize how badly it hurts to be insulted, or hit, or sexually tormented by someone who is supposed to care? Did you realize that love and romance can turn into a prison? It is painfully hard to see these things.

It took a lot of courage for you to pick up this book. It might be hard for you to read. You might see yourself in the girls or guys who talk about their experiences. It could be painful to find out that it is real, and it really is happening to you or someone you care about.

Reading this book is an important step. Maybe it's a beginning for you—to change your life, and your feelings about yourself. Maybe it's a beginning that will help you reach out to someone you care about.

Please note that we sometimes refer to the abuser as "he," because that is most common, but sometimes the abuser is a young woman. So as you read this book, keep in mind that the people you are reading about are in intimate relationships where a guy abuses his girlfriend, or a girl abuses her boyfriend, or a guy abuses his boyfriend, or a girl abuses her girlfriend.

"The first time it happened, I was about fourteen and my boyfriend was sixteen. He saw me hug my brother in

the hall at school, but he didn't know it was my brother because we'd just started dating. He dragged me out of school, behind a store and just beat me up—literally. He said if anyone asked me what happened, to tell them I got into a fight with someone; not to dare tell anyone he hit me."—Anonymous, 17

You may think you are the only one this is happening to. But that's not true. Many teenagers have problems with violence in a relationship with a boyfriend or girlfriend. Several surveys asked students in high school or college if they had been hit or sexually assaulted by someone they were dating or seeing. The surveys showed that an average of twenty-eight percent of the students experienced violence in a dating relationship.[1] That is more than one in every four students. In addition, studies show that sixty-seven percent of young women reporting rape were raped in dating situations.[2]

Dating violence is *serious*. Every abusive relationship has the possibility of ending in murder. An alarming number of young women are murdered by their boyfriends. According to the FBI, twenty percent of female homicide victims are between fifteen and twenty-four years old,[3] and one out of every three women murdered in the United States is killed by a husband or boyfriend.[4] Even if the abuser doesn't intend to kill his girlfriend, a hard shove or threats with a weapon can "accidentally" kill.

Dating violence occurs everywhere and to all kinds of people. There is no particular culture or community in which it occurs and others where it does not. This means that it happens in big cities and in small farming towns. It happens in wealthy neighborhoods and in housing projects. It happens in every culture and ethnic group. It happens in gay as well as straight relationships. It happens to teens who have babies and those who do not. Although it is more likely to happen to couples who live together, it often happens to those who do not.

It is most common for young women to be the victims and for the violent partner to be male. However, young women are also violent and young men are also victimized by dating violence.[5]

The majority of dating violence occurs when the relationship is serious or steady. In several studies, young men were more violent as they began to see themselves as part of a couple.[6] Some abusers become more violent when they think the relationship is going to end, or after their girlfriend or boyfriend does break up with them.

Do you believe that violence is a normal part of dating? Do you believe that hitting and jealousy are signs of love? Many teens believe this, even though it is not true.[7]

3 What Is Dating Violence?

"I've been with Carlos since I was thirteen.... He used to choke me, do awful things.... He used to make me feel that no one else would want me. I felt I better stay with him.... He scared me. Sometimes we would be driving somewhere, and all of a sudden he would take off with me in the car and drive to a parking place. Then he'd hit me because of something wrong I said. I was afraid of everything I said, afraid to say the wrong thing."—Consuela, 19

In a violent dating relationship, a person repeatedly threatens to, or actually acts in a way that physically, sexually or verbally injures their boyfriend or girlfriend. It does not just happen once, but happens again and again. It is *not* the same as getting angry or having fights. In a violent dating relationship, one person is afraid of and intimidated by the other.

Being abused by someone you love means being mistreated by them. This may be emotional or physical or sexual, or all three.

Emotional Abuse

Eighteen-year-old Sandy said:

"I was insulted, accused of crazy things, humiliated and had my mind twisted. I was constantly criticized and called names. I was put down, no, verbally attacked for things that were not a problem the day before. I was

blamed for everything that went wrong. Often, I had no idea what was wrong."

Sandy knew she was being hurt. She realized later that it has a name: emotional abuse.

Emotional abuse can be very confusing for teens. It is very confusing to be told you are worthless by the person who expresses such great love for you. One fourteen-year-old girl, who didn't want us to use her name, said:

"I figured maybe I did wear too much makeup, or maybe my skirt was too high, or maybe I really was a 'stupid, fucking bitch.' Maybe I did look like a whore or maybe I shouldn't have gone out with my friend.... Since I loved him, I figured, why would he lie to me? He loves me."

Jealousy and possessiveness are emotionally abusive. The abuser's jealousy and possessiveness give him control over the person he loves. For example, thirteen-year-old Salina described how the wonderful excitement of romance became controlling:

"We spent all our time together. It was wonderful at first, but it became obsessive. I was either with him or talking to him on the phone. He became more and more jealous. At one point, I even had to be on the phone with him when I went to sleep so that he knew I was at home at night. I was allowed to talk to only two people at school—both were girls, and he had his friends watch me to make sure I was obedient."

The abuser's jealousy and suspiciousness lead to accusations and intense questioning or interrogations. Jealousy leads to verbal harassment about everything you do or say—in the name of love. Jill was convinced that David loved her. She said:

"He often showed it through his extreme jealousy and possessiveness. I couldn't talk to another boy. . . . He resented my girlfriends and my family. He said, 'All we need is each other.' If he chose to go out with his friends or not bother to call me, I was supposed to sit at home and wait for him to call. If I wasn't there, I was interrogated over and over about where I was, who I talked to, even what I wore. The hassle wasn't worth it. I became more and more isolated, more dependent on David, and afraid of David's temper if I didn't do what he wanted."

The abuser's jealousy and anger can make it too frightening for you to do anything that will set him off. Sixteen-year-old Jim's girlfriend was terrified of his raging fits when he was jealous. He never hit her. He yelled at her, called her names, interrogated her for hours about everything she said or did with anybody. Later, after seeing a counselor, Jim said, "After a while, I got what I wanted: complete control over my girlfriend. Power."

Another way an abuser gets control with emotional abuse is by making a girlfriend or boyfriend feel crazy and doubt themselves. This could happen to you if you are threatened that your secrets or even lies about you will be revealed in school. If you are in a gay or lesbian relationship, your abuser may threaten to tell everyone at school that you are gay or a lesbian. Or your abuser may say one thing and do the opposite. Or say or do something, and then deny it, telling you that you are crazy or stupid.

Abusers also get control by using emotional abuse when they keep their girlfriend or boyfriend isolated. This could happen to you if you are being told that your friends and your family are no good, or if your abuser has a fit of rage every time you see a friend, or accuses you of betrayal if you talk about him or her to anyone else. Often it seems that your abuser sees your family, especially your parents, as an "enemy." If so, you may feel that if you talk to your parents you are being disloyal to your abuser.

Your things may have been thrown at you or destroyed. Thirteen-year-old Melanie repeatedly threatened her boyfriend, Brian, to try to control him. She verbally attacked him, or threw things when she didn't like something he did. For example, she broke Brian's Walkman when she picked it up and threw it against the wall across the room. She blew up because Brian was at the movies with his sister when she called earlier that day and wanted him to come over.

Emotional abuse destroys your independence. It makes you feel terrible about yourself. You begin to feel totally dependent on your abuser and that "no one else will ever want you." Felicia, who was eighteen, said:

> *"He beat me, but, you know, it was the verbal abuse that killed me the most. I just felt like I was no good, I was trash, the things he used to say to me...that I would never get another boyfriend in my life, that I'm a bitch, a whore."*

Physical Abuse

Physical abuse includes pushing, hitting, slapping, kicking, beatings with a fist, choking, attacks with an object or a weapon.

If you have been physically abused, you may have been restrained until you were bruised, or pulled by the hair. Sixteen-year-old Dawn grabbed her sixteen-year-old girlfriend, Cathy, by the arm and wouldn't let her leave. Later Cathy had huge bruises on her arm. Fourteen-year-old Tawnya's boyfriend, Todd, who was fifteen, yanked her head back by her hair in the hall at school after he saw her talking to a classmate.

Physical abuse is not a one-time incident. It is a pattern in the relationship, and *happens again and again.* Each time you are hit, it is worse than the time before.

Physical abuse is used to control you, to restrict you, to scare you.

Sexual Abuse

Sexual abuse is mistreatment by sexual acts, demands or insults.

You may have been violently forced to have sex. One fourteen-year-old girl described her experience:

> *"I was lying on the sofa crying, and he would stand over me, call me disgusting names, masturbate and ejaculate all over me. [Some]times he would tie me up.... Nothing felt good to me. All I ever did was lie there. I hated it, but usually I had no choice. Not once did sex even feel remotely good."*

You may not have been violently forced to have sex, but coerced or manipulated to have sex. What does "coerced" mean? Being coerced means being afraid to say no to sex. For example, you may not say no if you are afraid of being rejected, or if you are afraid of being hit. It means being manipulated so that you feel so bad about yourself or so afraid that you go along with sex when you don't want to. You may have been coerced to have sex by your boyfriend's threats to leave you, or by being made to feel inadequate or ugly.

Sixteen-year-old Luis would tell Kim, who was thirteen, that she looked fat, she really was ugly, but he put up with her. He wanted to have intercourse, and though she really liked Luis, she didn't want to have sex with him. Luis said it would really be too much for him to put up with her if she didn't. She felt ashamed, and was afraid she'd lose him. So she didn't stop him when he pushed her onto the bed and forced himself inside her, without caring about her feelings. The same thing happened again and again, and Kim felt more and more ashamed, and didn't realize until later that she was being sexually abused by coercion.

If you have refused to have sex or to do certain sexual acts, maybe you have been ignored. Seventeen-year-old Suzanne got sick at the thought of oral sex, and even though she said no, eighteen-year-old Brad would push her head down on him and wouldn't let her up until she "did it."

You may have been forced to have sex with others, or to watch your boyfriend or girlfriend have sex with someone else. You may have been humiliated or insulted sexually, so that you feel ashamed, or you feel that there is something wrong with you. Nineteen-year-old Jon used to point to guys on the street and tell seventeen-year-old Manny how good the other guys look, and how ugly he is, and how Manny doesn't give him good enough sex. He'd say to him, in front of their friends, that he wants to do it with this guy or that guy, because Manny's no good.

You may have been forced to have sex without protection from pregnancy or AIDS. Joan, who was sixteen, said:

"I listened to everything Jeff said when it came to sex, because he was the first guy I was with. Whenever I asked him to use a condom, he refused. He said it 'ruined his pleasure.' He told me in this mean way that I couldn't satisfy him, and made me feel ugly. I'd cry. He'd lie, and say he had an AIDS test and I shouldn't worry. Or he'd say that his doctor told him he can't have children, so we didn't need birth control. I realized it wasn't true when I got pregnant. I had an abortion, which was the hardest thing I have ever had to do."

■ **When asked, "What are some of the ways you have been EMOTIONALLY ABUSED?" teens answered:**

- *yelled at*
- *money stolen*
- *constantly blamed for partner's own faults*
- *verbally harassed*

- *called names*
- *constantly accused of flirting or having sex with others*
- *repeatedly interrogated*

- *publicly humiliated*
- *treasured possessions broken*
- *labeled "stupid" or "crazy"*

■ **When asked, "What are some of the ways you have been PHYSICALLY ABUSED?" teens answered:**

- *scratched*
- *choked*
- *hair pulled*
- *cut with knife*
- *kicked in stomach when pregnant*

- *held arm so tight it bruised*
- *hit head against wall*
- *slapped*
- *punched in face, arm*

- *arm twisted*
- *hit with object*
- *beat up*
- *fingers bent*
- *dumped out of car*
- *burned*

■ **When asked, "What are some of the ways you have been SEXUALLY ABUSED?" teens answered:**

- *called sexual names*
- *wanted sex after hitting*
- *made me walk home nude*
- *always wanted sex, mad when I didn't want to*
- *forced sex*
- *forced me to do "disgusting" sex acts*
- *bit, pinched breast*

- *acted indifferent*
- *threatened to get a new woman*
- *raped*
- *slapped, pinched to get his way*
- *forced me to have sex without protection*

Exercise

Use this blank page to write down any of the ways you think your boyfriend or girlfriend has been *emotionally or verbally abusive* to you. Write the ways you think they have been *physically abusive*. Write down the ways you think they have been *sexually abusive*. Write about how you feel after reading this section.

4 How Can You Tell if Your Relationship Is Abusive?

For Victims

"I had no idea I was being abused. Then my mother showed me a book and I read other girls' stories of their abuse. I realized what they were saying was happening to me. Before that I kept justifying everything he did to me. It changed my thinking from "What did I do wrong?" to "I don't deserve to be treated like this."
—*Sandra, 19*

Many victims don't recognize that they are being abused. They don't realize how they have gradually changed because of the abuse. Are you a victim of dating violence? Answer the questions below. If you answer yes to two or more of them, you are in an abusive relationship, or your relationship is likely to become abusive.

■Are You a Victim of Dating Violence?

- *Are you frightened of your boyfriend or girlfriend's temper?*
- *Are you afraid to disagree with him or her?*
- *Do you find yourself apologizing to yourself or others for your boyfriend or girlfriend's behavior when you are treated badly?*

- *Have you been frightened by his or her violence towards others?*
- *Have you been hit, kicked, shoved or had things thrown at you?*
- *Do you not see friends or family because of his or her jealousy?*
- *Have you been forced to have sex?*
- *Have you been afraid to say no to sex?*
- *Are you forced to justify everything you do, every place you go and every person you see to avoid his or her temper?*
- *Have you been wrongly and repeatedly accused of flirting or having sex with others?*
- *Are you unable to go out, get a job or go to school without his or her permission?*
- *Have you become secretive, ashamed or hostile to your parents because of this relationship?*

For Abusers

> "Getting locked up for my violence has helped me to confront my problem. Before that I threatened my girlfriend verbally, and I smashed her hand into a wall. I pushed, grabbed, shook her and put a gun to her head."
> —Allen, 18

If you are emotionally or verbally abusive, you may believe that you are also a victim. You may believe that others cause your problems, and cause your violence. The result is that you don't recognize that you have a problem that only *you* can change. Answer the questions below. If you answer yes to two or more of these, then you are an abuser.

■*Are You an Abuser?*

- *Are you extremely jealous and possessive?*
- *Do you have an explosive temper?*
- *Do you consistently ridicule, criticize or insult your girlfriend or boyfriend?*
- *Do you become violent when you drink and/or use drugs?*
- *Have you broken their things or thrown things at them?*
- *Have you hit, pushed, kicked or otherwise injured them when you were angry?*
- *Have you threatened to hurt or kill them or someone close to them?*
- *Have you forced them to have sex, or intimidated them so they are afraid to say no?*
- *Have you threatened to kill yourself if they leave?*
- *Do you make them account to you for every moment they are away from you?*
- *Do you spy on them or call them constantly to check up on them?*
- *Do you accuse them of seeing other guys or girls?*

---

5 The Cycle of Violence

"One small disagreement would lead to another....
[It] would build to a crescendo, which always ended
with...Mike's violence. Then the storm would clear,
and we would make up passionately and be happy for
days or weeks until the next storm started to build."
—Marge, 18

If you are in a violent relationship it will get worse unless something changes—unless the person who is violent
takes active steps to change, or unless the victim leaves.

You may have noticed that there is a pattern, a cycle in
your relationship. Abusers seem to be like two different
people: loving some of the time, and cruel some of the time.
Their behavior and mood go back and forth in repeated cycles. As time passes, the cycles get shorter and shorter. For
many abusers, the **honeymoon** stage eventually stops, and
they go back and forth between **tension-building** and **explosion**.

Dana and Jason are both sixteen years old. They go to
the same high school. They have been going together for
eight months, and going through the stages in the cycle of
violence. Their experience is typical of abusive dating relationships.

The Tension-Building Stage

During the **tension-building** stage, Jason becomes more
and more temperamental, edgy, critical and explosive. He

blows up over little things, throws things, constantly criticizes Dana. He "punishes" her for "mistakes." He blames her for anything he feels is wrong—no matter what she does.

Jason is jealous and possessive. He accuses Dana of dressing too sexy, or flirting, or having sex with others. He calls her constantly to see where she is—or to make sure she doesn't go anywhere.

Sometimes, Dana thinks Jason's demands are flattering. They seem to prove his love. She knows she is important to him. But little by little, Dana has become more and more afraid of doing something that will trigger his temper.

During the tension-building stage, Dana becomes very careful. She is afraid to do anything she believes will make Jason become violent. She tries to keep the peace, to please him. When he wants to know where she's been, she tries to tell him the truth. Then she tries to tell him what she thinks he wants to hear. When he gets mad at what she says, she tries to explain. After a while she realizes it doesn't matter what she says. Jason twists whatever she says so that he just gets angrier and angrier. When she tries to calm him down or humor him, or gets quiet just to get it over with, he keeps building his anger up to an explosion point.

Sometimes it just ends as suddenly as it started, or he says he wouldn't get this way if he knew she loved him. Then he wants to have sex. When he is like that, sex isn't fun, because Jason is trying to prove something, and he's rough with her.

He calms down a little, but the tension is still there. And Dana keeps watching him, trying to avoid fights. She becomes tense and nervous. She gets terrible stomach aches; her doctor thinks she is developing an ulcer. Sometimes she gets sick. She is usually a happy person, full of energy, but when the tension between her and Jason gets bad, she becomes withdrawn and depressed. She watches Jason closely, and forgets to take care of herself, so she goes to school in her oldest or dirtiest clothes. She gets so distracted with worry about Jason, that she can't concentrate in school, and although she is usually a good student, she forgets her assignments and fails exams.

The Explosion Stage

The tension-building stage ends with a violent **explosion**. The abuser verbally and/or physically attacks his girlfriend. Usually it is more severe than abuse during the tension-building stage, or worse than previous explosions.

Jason's anger builds, and he stops trying to cool off. He lets it go and lashes out at Dana. He calls her names, hits her, and won't let her get away from him. Then suddenly, his tension is released. It's over (until the next time). Afterwards, he always feels sorry, and is afraid that Dana will leave him. He has given her a black eye and bruises, and when he sees how he has hurt her, he cries and begs her to forgive him.

Dana tries to get away from Jason before he explodes, and sometimes she can, but other times she can't. It is a relief for her too when it is over. But it also makes her angry. No matter what she does, Jason hurts her. A couple of times, after he has beaten her up, she has broken up with him.

The "Honeymoon" Stage

The third stage, the **honeymoon** stage that follows the explosion, is what keeps the couple together. Jason is apologetic, romantic, passionate. He promises to change and never hurt her again. Dana is hurt and wants to get away from him. But he is so much like his old self, and he feels so bad, she remembers the things she loves about him when he is not abusive. She knows he loves her, and that he needs her.

They become loving again, and Jason is not so tense, but fun to be with again. Dana feels relieved, her energy is high again, and she feels better. Jason doesn't feel so easily irritated and jealous, and doesn't seem to twist everything Dana says or does any more. They go to their special places, and enjoy their time together.

They both find excuses for his "blow-up"—his unhappy childhood, his failures in school, her failure to keep him happy. They may even think that his violence was justified or deserved. They deny the fact that the violence is Jason's problem. He doesn't control *himself* and *his* temper. They both begin to believe that the violence was a "misunderstanding" and won't happen again . . . until the tension begins to build again . . .

The Cycle of Violence

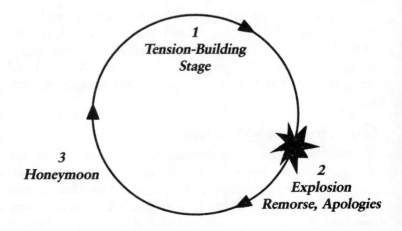

Exercise

Use this blank page to write about how you are feeling or to make notes for yourself.

6 Why Do Guys Abuse Their Girlfriends?

"My mom's boyfriend hit me to teach me to be tough. My mom used to hit me and when I get angry I hit in any kind of situation. I enjoyed intimidating people."
—*Ray, 18*

It is hard to explain why a person might be cruel or violent to someone they love. There is no single explanation for it. There are several factors that contribute to violence in relationships.

Jealousy

Many high school and college students say that jealousy is the major cause of dating violence. Although it is based on insecurity, teens often think jealousy is a sign of love. The abuser says, "I love you so much I can't stand for you to have other friends. I want you all to myself." A girlfriend or boyfriend feels flattered by this proof of love.

But they may ignore the way jealousy leads the abuser to restrict and control her or him, and to hit and be violent. What starts out as romance and "special" love becomes a prison for the person who is loved. Love becomes a prison when an abusive boyfriend says to his girlfriend, "I want you all to myself," and then has jealous, angry explosions when his girlfriend sees her friends or does something she wants to do for herself. Then, because she is afraid, the abuser's girlfriend tries to avoid the abuser's bad temper and violence. So gradually, she stops doing things or seeing people that are important to her. She becomes more isolated, and more dependent on the abuser as the only person in her life. And the abuser becomes *more* jealous and violent, *not* less. That is because he discovers that his jealousy gives him an excuse to control the person he loves, by keeping her intimidated, frightened and dependent on him. (This also applies to girls who control their boyfriends with jealousy, and to gay relationships as well.)

In fact, jealousy does *not* really come from loving feelings. People are jealous because they are insecure about themselves, and they are afraid they won't be loved. Because they are insecure, they use their jealousy to dominate and control the person they love.

Using Violence to Assert Power

In our society, teenagers can learn mistaken ideas of what is normal in a relationship from what they see in movies, television and advertising. They see many situations in which a strong person or group maintains their power by using violence to control people who are less powerful. For example, they see bigger or older kids bully smaller or younger kids. They see governments use armies or bombs when they have a conflict. They see women treated badly in the movies or on TV. Then they see that people think it's romantic or funny or not serious. They may see adults they know using violence to show they have power. So they assume that maintaining power with violence is normal.

Not Treating Women with Respect

Young men often believe it is their right to abuse a woman. They may mistakenly believe that men should dominate and control women, and that women are passive, stupid and obligated to please men.

There is a lot of peer pressure on guys to be sexually active, so sometimes they are sexually aggressive with girls. Guys feel it is their role to be dominant and to control their girlfriends' activities and behavior.

Guys get approval from their friends for being "the boss," for keeping their girlfriend "in line" by pushing her around, or for ignoring her when she says no to sex. They may be afraid they won't look "man enough" if they don't behave this way.

Girls feel pressured to do what their boyfriends want them to do, even if it hurts them. Girls often learn to be dependent on their boyfriends. They learn to put him first, and not have anything important in their lives apart from the relationship. They are judgmental and critical of girls who are not seeing one special guy. A girl feels peer pressure to be in a relationship even if it is not good for her.

Girls feel pressured to have sex when they don't want to. A girl may blame herself if her boyfriend makes her have sex in spite of her saying no. The pressure comes from mistaken ideas about sex and about relationships. For example, teenagers often believe that if a guy takes a girl out, she is "obligated" to have sex with him, even if she doesn't want to. Many teenagers believe that guys are justified in raping a girl if they are turned on by her or if they have spent money on her. Once a girl agrees to have sex with her boyfriend, she may believe that she doesn't have the right to say no, or to change her mind or not want to do particular sex acts, or she may believe she doesn't have the right to say no on another date—as if he "owns" her. Or she may be afraid that she will lose her "reputation," and be seen as a "slut" by other teens if she doesn't agree to his "ownership" of her.

These beliefs contribute to dating violence.

•

Violence During Childhood

Young men who were abused as children or who saw their mothers being abused are more likely to abuse their girlfriends, wives or children. They have learned from their abusive parent to blame others for their problems. They have learned to release their tension by exploding and losing their temper, no matter who gets hurt. They have not learned other ways to handle their problems and feelings. They have not learned to treat women with respect.

Difficulty Handling Insecurity or Anger

Guys or girls who are violent with their girlfriends or boyfriends have trouble handling their insecurities and fears. They are afraid their girlfriend or boyfriend will leave them, so they have trouble trusting them. They also have trouble controlling their anger. They blame their girlfriends or boyfriends when they lose their temper. They don't know how to communicate or to talk about their feelings. They don't empathize or understand how their girlfriends or boyfriends can feel afraid and upset when they get angry and treat them badly.

Alcohol and Drugs

Many teenagers who have experienced violence say that drinking and using drugs make it worse. It doesn't *cause* violence. But drinking or using drugs allows a person to let down inhibitions and become violent.

For example, a guy gets drunk at a party and after the party takes his girlfriend home and verbally and physically attacks her. At the party, he is able to decide *not* to beat up other people. He has saved it for his girlfriend. If he had decided not to drink, he might have been able to decide not to beat up his girlfriend, too. So he uses his drinking as an excuse to be violent towards his girlfriend.

Abusing alcohol and drugs are often dangerous ways of avoiding personal problems.

■ When asked why they abused their girlfriends, guys answered:

- *I'd get jealous. I'd get crazy if she looked at anyone else. If she dressed pretty, the way I like, I'd be out of my mind because I'd think everybody's looking at her.*
- *My dad beat up on my mom.*
- *I had a hard time trusting anyone, especially girls.*
- *I kept thinking she would leave me and I'd go crazy. I wouldn't want her to get to me like that. So I wouldn't let her do anything without my permission.*
- *I felt powerless as a child in my family and I wanted power so I took it—in my gang and with my girlfriend.*
- *Jealousy.*
- *I have bad anger flashes. I can't control my anger.*
- *I felt bad about myself. I get violent if I can't trust.*
- *Alcohol and drugs.*
- *I was a victim of emotional and physical abuse and I have a hot temper.*
- *I felt I had to be tough, to be a man. I thought my girlfriend was pushing me around, controlling me. Now I know it wasn't right.*
- *I get violent when I drink, but I didn't stop drinking.*

---

7 Romantic, Nurturing and Addictive Love

"He had to have my attention whenever he wanted it. He expected me to wait around for him when he was busy. He called me in the middle of the night if he wanted to tell me something. One day I found out he was cheating on me, and that he lied to me about a lot of things. He told me it was my fault. That night, I was begging him to give me a second chance. I asked him what I could do to make him want me. I was terrified of losing him."—Sandra, 19

You meet each other, you like each other, you find each other exciting and fun. You fall in love.

Love can be nurturing, romantic or addictive. What kind of love do you have?

Romantic Love

Almost all relationships start with **romantic love**. In romantic love, everything seems perfect, as if you have found *the one* person who is just right for you. You can only see the good things about each other. Things you don't like you think of as positive. For example, later you might think she is "selfish," but at the peak of romance, she is not selfish, just "forgetful." Later, you might think he is "domineering" or "possessive," but at the peak of romance, he is "devoted" and "loving."

Romantic love is thrilling, exciting, passionate. You forget about everyone else in the world but your new love. You do special things together, buy each other things, write passionate letters, talk on the phone for hours.

As you spend more time together, and get to know one another, your new relationship starts to fit into your usual way of life. You see your friends again. You focus on school again. You survive your first disagreement, and begin to realize that sometimes you see things differently. You find out that there are things you don't like about each other.

Some couples decide not to continue seeing each other, because they realize that this isn't what they want after all, and they really aren't a good match. Couples that do continue seeing each other find ways to work out their differences, and to love each other after the romance of the beginning wears off.

As the romantic love gradually changes, and it always does, love becomes either **nurturing** or **addictive**. There can still be romance and passion between you, but it is part, not all, of what you have together.

As you are reading this, you may be thinking, "romantic love is so great! That's the kind of love *I* want!" Romantic love is exciting at the beginning, but it is **nurturing love** that lasts a long time and makes a couple feel good being together.

Nurturing Love

If you and your boyfriend or girlfriend have **nurturing love** for each other, you both wish for the other to grow and be happy. You wish for the other to be everything they are capable of being. You encourage each other to have friends and to enjoy activities that you do separately as well as those you do together. You support each other to do well in school or at work. You feel safe to express your feelings. If you have an argument, neither of you is afraid of the other. You are comfortable being yourself.

If one of you wants time alone, the other can accept it. What if one of you wants to end a relationship based on nurturing love, and the other is not ready? The one being left feels sad, upset, and may have a difficult time for a while. But being left, you do not feel self-destructive, as if your life is over.

Mary and Steve met at a friend's party, and within a week, they were seeing each other every day. They laughed a lot. Everything they did together seemed special. They were in love. For three weeks, they passed notes to each other in school, walked home together, did homework and watched TV together, talked on the phone from the time they each went to their own houses until they went to sleep at night. When they had been together almost a month, Mary told Steve that she was going out with a group of her friends on Friday night. She had also been missing pep team practice to be with him, and she didn't want to be kicked out. Steve had wanted to see Mary Friday night, but he told her, "Go and enjoy yourself. Friends are important." When she told him about pep team practice, he was relieved, because he had been missing the pick-up basketball games he had stopped when he met Mary. They continued to see each other a lot, but they gradually got back into the groove of their usual activities and friends.

They had a big fight when Steve didn't want to take Mary's little sister with them one Saturday night. They both felt terrible, and were afraid they were going to break up over it. Mary thought Steve didn't understand about being in a big family because he wasn't in one. Although Steve continued to hate it when Mary wanted to bring any of her sisters along on their dates, they worked it out. Every now and then (not every week), they took one of her sisters out, and brought her home in the middle of the evening so they still had time alone together. They disagreed about other things too. But they were crazy about each other, and as time passed, they liked each other more and more. Their relationship made the change from **romantic** to **nurturing** love.

Addictive Love

Addictive love can lead to trouble. You are "addicted" if one or both of you believe you cannot live without the other. Feeling intensely romantic after you first meet, you want to be together every minute. Then gradually you feel more desperate to be together, as if you need each other, and are terrified of being alone. You find yourself doing things that aren't good for you so that you can be together. Anything your boyfriend or girlfriend does apart from you threatens you, as if you are going to lose him or her if you aren't together constantly.

Guys may hide feelings like this from their girlfriends, because they think it isn't manly to feel you "need" a girl. So a guy expresses these needs by being controlling and critical. For example, he might demand that his girlfriend have nothing in her life but him. He tells her that she is not good enough as a woman or as a girlfriend, and he makes her feel dependent on him.

Not every addictive relationship is abusive. But relationships like this are more at risk for abuse. If you are abusive, you take advantage of your girlfriend's or boyfriend's addictive need for you, and use force to control her or him. If you have addictive love for your girlfriend (or boyfriend), you will do anything to keep her (or him) from leaving, including making her (or him) afraid to leave.

If you are the abused girlfriend or boyfriend, your addiction can lead you to ignore or excuse the violence. You may be afraid he or she will leave you, and become afraid to be alone. If you don't leave the relationship or if you don't object to the way you are being treated, your abuser may think he or she has permission to be more abusive. You become a handy target when your abuser is upset with anything in his or her life.

Debbie and Lenny lived a block apart, but didn't really know each other because they went to different schools. But one day they were hanging out with kids in the neighborhood, and they were flirting and having a good time. Lenny asked Debbie out, and before he knew it, Debbie was calling him constantly, giving him poems and talking about their future together.

Lenny thought Debbie was the most beautiful and exciting girl he had ever met, but he was a little scared because things were happening so fast. He told Debbie he wanted to slow down a little, go out together with friends, and have some time apart from each other so they could keep up in school. Debbie got upset, and asked if he was trying to break up with her. When he said, "Not at all!" she said she couldn't see why they ever had to be apart.

When Lenny made plans to play ball with his friends, Debbie called him six times before he left his house and after he got home. She needed to know that he missed her, because she didn't think she could live without him. Lenny started feeling overwhelmed, although he loved her, and he told her they should not see each other for a few days. He got the scare of his life when Debbie called in the middle of the next night saying she was going to kill herself because he didn't love her any more.

Lenny and Debbie's relationship made the transition from **romantic** to **addictive** love.

●

■ *Signs of Addictive Love:*

- *You believe you can't live without her or him.*
- *You have fewer and fewer happy times together, and more and more time spent on apologies, promises, anger, guilt and fear.*
- *You feel worse about yourself.*
- *You feel you have less and less self-control.*
- *You don't make decisions or plans, waiting to find out what he or she is going to do.*
- *You enjoy time away from him or her less and less, as if you are killing time until you can be together again.*
- *You keep breaking your promises to yourself to be less desperate ("I won't call him"; "I won't make her tell me everything she did since I saw her").*
- *You feel you can never get enough of her or him.*
- *You try more and more to control her or him.*

Exercise

Use this blank page to write about your relationship. Is your love addictive? Write about your feelings or make notes for yourself.

8 *The Scars Caused by Dating Violence*

"She was worried all the time and she lost a lot of weight, not like she was fat or anything, and she didn't see a lot of her old friends. We [her friends] drifted away for a while."—Rosa, 18

"I was blond, green-eyed and 130 pounds. I competed in gymnastics—until I quit because he wanted to spend more time with me. After two years with Andy, I weighed over 250 pounds. I never left my house. My education had been suffering. I had one girlfriend with whom I spoke, and that was it."—Anonymous, 14

"I started feeling real inadequate. My grades went down dramatically. I missed class a lot, because I felt sick—stomach stuff, real nervous stuff. . . . It was probably a deep depression, but I started feeling sleepy all the time, all I wanted to do was stay in bed. It just seemed like everything just kept going down, down, down."
—Anonymous, 19

If you are being abused, or if you were abused in the past, you are a *survivor*. You are reading this book. You are asking questions. You have gotten through moments of feeling you might not live, or of feeling hopeless and totally bad about yourself. Yet you kept finding hope and strength. You find ways to fight to keep yourself going, to protect and take care of yourself.

Sometimes you might think that this is no big deal. You

might forget about your strength, and think of yourself as weak. But you must be strong to be here reading this book today. And you are helping yourself to begin to heal.

Verbal insults and name-calling, hitting, being forced or coerced to have sex when you don't want to: these hurt. They cause long-lasting physical and emotional effects. You may be feeling some of the effects of the violence in your relationship. Do you have any of the following?

Physical Scars

Do you have scars from injuries? Do you have bruises or broken bones? Do you have stitches? Do you have a permanent disability from the physical abuse, such as a hearing loss or paralysis?

Neglected Appearance

To avoid triggering your boyfriend's or girlfriend's jealousy, do or did you neglect your appearance? Do you dress in baggy, unattractive clothes? Are you afraid to look attractive? If you have been sexually abused, do you hate yourself and your body? Have you gained or lost a lot of weight, because of the stress and nervousness caused by being abused?

Shame

Do you feel ashamed, as if there is something terribly wrong with you because this happened to you? Do you blame yourself for the abuse? Do you now question yourself, your decisions, your abilities, your appearance—and you didn't before the abusive relationship?

Fear

Are you fearful or nervous a lot of the time? Do you get a stomach ache when you hear people arguing? Do you panic when you see someone who reminds you of your abuser? Do you have nightmares or flashbacks about the violent things that were done to you? Are you terrified of making mistakes or saying the wrong thing—no matter who you are with?

Do you find yourself thinking about your abusive boyfriend or girlfriend all the time, because you have a habit of watching him or her closely?

If you have broken up with your abusive boyfriend or girlfriend, are you afraid that he or she will try to hurt you? Has he or she threatened to in the past ("If you ever leave..."), or is he or she still threatening or harassing you?

Isolation

Are you isolated and alone? Have you lost your friendships and your closeness to your family because your boyfriend or girlfriend demanded it? Did you start to feel ashamed, and withdraw even more from your family and friends? Are you afraid to see your friends now, because you are afraid they won't believe you? Are you afraid that they think you caused the abuse? Are you afraid your friends won't understand about the closeness and intense bond that kept you together even though he or she was violent?

Protective Feelings

Do you feel that you protect your relationship with your abuser, even when it is not good for you to do so? Do you feel paranoid at times, not trusting anyone, or afraid of people interfering?

Depression

Are you depressed? If you are depressed, you might answer "yes" to the following questions. Do you feel as if you have no energy, or you're tired all the time? Are you tearful, or do your emotions go up and down too much? Do you sleep too much, or have trouble sleeping? Has your eating changed and have you gained or lost a lot of weight without wanting to? Do you have trouble thinking about the future? Do you think about yourself and your life as worthless? Do you think about dying or killing yourself?

Exercise

Use this blank page to write about your scars, or if you are an abuser, the scars you have caused your boyfriend or girlfriend.

9 *Healing From Abuse*

If you are feeling any of the effects of being in a violent relationship that are mentioned in this book, or if you are feeling others that are not mentioned here, *you need time and support to heal*. You have been hurt—physically and emotionally. It takes time to feel like yourself again. It takes support from parents and family members, from friends, from counseling, from others who have had similar experiences. It takes being around people who are *not* abusive so that you can feel the difference, and feel safe to be yourself again. You can use strength you have used to survive in the relationship to do things that make you feel good about yourself again, and to heal. When you are out of the relationship, you can focus that strength on yourself (rather than on dealing with your abuser).

Even though violence may have some long-lasting effects, you *can* heal from them. You *can* feel like yourself again, and you can feel happy and trusting again. It takes courage—like the courage it has taken for you to read this book. Say to yourself, "I have courage. I *will* heal and be happy again."

10 *Break Up or Stay?*

"My reasons for staying with him, I see, were very stupid reasons. I found myself hanging onto the boyfriend I had met at first, the nice one, instead of realizing that this might be a different person now—a violent one, a drug addict. This one beat me up. I just wanted to hang on to the nice one."—Catherine, 17

"Mostly I was afraid of what she would do. My biggest thought was that she was going to change and that I was strong and good enough that I could help her change."—Chris, 18

"I started trying to break up with him. But he would come to me crying, 'I love you. I'll never hurt you again.' When I'd see him cry, I'd remember the softness and gentleness he could show. It would give me hope that we could work it out. I'd leave him and go back.... When [his crying] didn't work, he started threatening to hurt me and my friends and my mom. It even got to the point where he threatened to commit suicide."—Salina, 13

Being in an abusive relationship is overwhelming. You wake up in the morning saying to yourself, "This is the last time I'm going to take this!" Then you think, "But I don't want to be alone!" Or you think, "My baby won't have his father!" And some mornings you wake up and say, "I love him! I'm not going to take this, but I'm not going to break up with him either!"

Why It Is Hard To Decide

Victims usually try to find some way of getting away from the violence without having to break up. You may be clear that you want the violence to stop. No one *chooses* to be in a violent relationship. No one likes to be called names, accused of awful things, hit or raped. But you may not be at all clear about wanting the relationship to end. Making a decision to change your life is challenging. It is empowering. It is also frightening, and hard to do. It takes a lot of courage to change your life.

There are so many reasons you might be afraid to end the violent relationship. Are you afraid of being alone? Are you afraid because your boyfriend or girlfriend becomes more threatening or violent when the subject of breaking up comes up? Are you afraid you will never find someone to love you again? If your relationship has been sexual, are you afraid you will be seen as a "slut"? Are you overwhelmed by how hard it would be to stay away from him or her, or to convince him or her to stay away from you? Do you feel you don't deserve (or won't get) anything better? Of course you are afraid to leave! You are afraid it will be as hard to leave as it is to stay and be hurt.

While it may *feel* just as hard to leave as it is to stay, it is far more dangerous to stay. It will hurt you more in the long run to stay and be repeatedly abused.

You deserve to be treated lovingly—and respectfully. It is *your* life, and you deserve to be in charge of it. You are strong, and courageous—look what you have already been through!

•

■ When asked why they stayed and didn't get out of a violent relationship right away, girls answered:

- *I really loved him (when he was not being violent) and hoped he would change.*
- *I felt I was the only one who understood him—he needed me. I felt I could help him.*
- *He'd cry and promise not to do it again. I believed it.*
- *My friends think he's great, and, ashamed to admit we had problems, I kept trying to make things work.*
- *I was afraid of him because he threatened to hurt or kill me, or other guys I might go out with.*
- *I felt lucky to have him, and believed that no one else would want to be with me; I was convinced that I was ugly, stupid.*
- *We go to the same school. I was pressured by his friends, like I was doing something terrible to him when I told him I wanted to break up.*
- *I believed that everything would be fine when his problems were solved, for example, when he didn't have pressure from parents or school.*
- *I believed that the violence would stop when we lived together or got married because then he would trust me.*
- *I have tried to break up, but he harassed me or became so depressed he scared me, so I tried to keep things calm until the "right" time.*
- *I had a baby with him. How could I break up with the father of my kid?*

What Has Led Girls to Decide to Break Up?

Teens who break up with their abusive boyfriends or girlfriends have different reasons for finally making the decision. Often they decide to leave several times before they actually break it off permanently.

What led them to decide to break up?

• *Finally believing they didn't deserve to be treated badly*

"It made a difference to hear from my friends and family members (my sisters, my brother, my parents) and others that I didn't deserve to be treated badly."

"When the police and the principal at school and the courts responded to what was happening to me, and said that this was a serious crime, I realized how badly I was being hurt."

"When I heard it enough times, I finally believed it: what was happening to me was wrong, I was being emotionally and physically hurt, and I didn't deserve it."

• *Violence got worse*

"I realized it wasn't going to get better, that the abuse was getting worse."

"Something snapped for me when Richard broke my nose. Deep inside I knew that if he broke my nose, something worse would be next."

"I suddenly stopped hoping he would change. And when I realized that he won't change, I couldn't love him any more."

• *Realizing they were losing too much*

"All of a sudden I realized that I was losing too much."

"I realized that my son was being damaged by seeing his mother get hit."

"I was planning to go to college and I had hopes for the future. But I realized that my boyfriend wasn't allowing me to have hopes and plans because of his jealousy."

"There were lots of things to enjoy that I had missed because of the abusive relationship. I wanted the freedom to do things my friends do, that other teens do. I wanted to meet new people, go places, participate at school, do things with friends and with my sisters and brothers."

• *Hitting bottom*

"I realized that I was being dragged down. I hit bottom, and I decided to survive—and that meant leaving my boyfriend."

"I looked at myself, and realized I was becoming something I hated. I had to leave my boyfriend, and I had to stop doing drugs and drinking."

• *Realizing they couldn't stop the violence*

"I saw my boyfriend hitting and being mean to a girl he was seeing when he was cheating on me. I realized that it wasn't me, or anything I did. There wasn't anything special or bad about me that made him violent. Then I realized I had to get away from his violence—nothing I could do would ever change it."

• *Support from family and friends*

"Friends and family who were encouraging and supportive helped me decide to leave."

"My friends confronted my abuser."

"My family helped me to protect myself from my abuser. They listened."

• *New, hopeful perspectives*

"I read a story in the newspaper about a girl who was abused by her boyfriend, and I knew that was what was happening to me. I realized I could get out of this. I felt hopeful."

"In a class I took we did reading about women and girls

and relationships, and we discussed things that helped me understand what was happening to me. It made me stronger."

Almost all teens who leave do it because they get to a point where they feel stronger and able to live without their abuser. They think about the future, and the kind of life they want to have, a life without abuse. And they feel hopeful that they can have that life. This is a new perspective, a new way of seeing themselves. And when they feel hopeful, they feel strong enough to leave, and build a new life without abuse.

Exercise

Use this blank page to write about your feelings or to make notes for yourself. What makes (or made) it difficult for you to leave your relationship if it is (or was) abusive?

11 *What Can You Do If You Are Being Abused?*

"I never told anybody about it. Because I was ashamed. Now I can talk about it. Before, it hurt too bad, I didn't want to remember. I had nightmares about it. I tried to hide it from my mom. My mom and I are close, but there's some things that you can't talk about. But I figure from the very first time that he had hit me, if I had told my mom, there wouldn't have been another time—because he knew the consequences he'd have to face."
—Anonymous, 18

"It made a difference to have the police and courts stop him. He came out of jail and we talked things out. He hasn't hit me since."—Consuela, 19

"[I finally attended a school in a different city.] Away from our abusive fights, I was able to build my self-reliance in small ways. I learned to have fun without Mike, to make decisions . . . and to [be okay without] seeing him every day. Slowly, I built my self-confidence. I defined myself on my own terms, rather than seeing myself as Mike's girlfriend. . . . His own behavior also helped me break away from him. Although he started dating someone else, I still found it difficult to stay away from him. He became more and more violent. He smashed his fist through his new girlfriend's wall. I had believed until then that I was the only woman who could really 'drive' him to violence."—Marge, 19

"[I told my social worker at the health clinic.] I told her because she always listened. She didn't blame me—for being pregnant or for him beating on me. It was a relief, because no one else believed it was happening. I told her because I was sick of it. But it was hard. It hurt a lot to talk about it. It made it real. But deep down inside, I was a really hurt person. When I told her, I believed it. What helped was a lot of counseling and a lot of friends telling me I was not a bad person. I had to hear it a lot of times, LOTS OF TIMES, but then I heard it."
—Felicia, 18

You deserve safety. You deserve love that doesn't hurt so much. You deserve to wake up every morning and feel free, not afraid.

You have a lot of strength. Remember the times you have been strong in dealing with being abused:

• Remember the times you said something or did something that kept you from being hurt worse.

• Remember the times you told someone about it.

• Remember the ways you have avoided the violence.

• Remember how you have kept going when you have felt so much fear and pain.

When you think about how you have survived the emotional pain and the physical injuries, are you surprised to realize how strong you are?

You can use your strength to plan for your safety and freedom from violence.

Look in a mirror. Say to yourself in the mirror, "You deserve to be loved without being hurt! You are strong and courageous! You are a survivor!"

Have your friends, your parents, and others all given you the same advice: "Get out! Break up with your abuser!"? This often happens to victims of abuse. People see the abuse, and don't understand the rest. They don't understand that you don't want the abuse, but you do want the love, and you do want the way it feels when it's good between you. Or they may not understand that you have been trying to break up, but it gets too scary, because he (or she) won't let you go.

When you saw the title of this section, **What Can You Do?**, did you say to yourself, "I know, they're going to say 'Break up with him (or her)', just like everyone else"?

As we said in the last section, this is a very difficult decision. The pull to be with your abuser and the urge to get away from him or her are both powerful. If you haven't decided yet whether to leave or to stay in the relationship, there are still things you can do to be safe and to protect yourself from the violence.

If you *have* decided to end the relationship, but have been afraid to do it, there are things you can do to be safe and to protect yourself from the violence while you are breaking up and afterwards. You probably know by now that your abuser gets more violent when he or she believes that you are leaving him or her.

If you have broken up, there are things you can do to be safe, and to heal from the effects of the abuse.

Remember:

If you decide to leave, or
if you decide to stay, or
if you decide to think about it for a while longer, or
if you have already left,
you are strong, and you can be safe and protect yourself from violence.

•

Things You Can Do to Be Safe

How can you be safe? How can you cope? How can you begin to recover from the emotional and physical damage the abuse has caused you? How can you be free from the violence?

• **Take it seriously.** Let your abuser know that emotional, sexual and physical abuse are all *serious and dangerous*. You don't deserve it. Make it clear you won't allow it. If you insist that they go for counseling or Alcoholics Anonymous, or that they change their behavior, be ready to follow through on your threat or promise. If you say you'll leave if they don't change, but you don't leave when they continue their old behavior, they will think they have your permission to continue the violence.

• **Plan for your safety.** If you are *not* ready to break up, think of a safety plan for when they are violent. If you *are* ready to break up, think of a safety plan for their explosive reaction or harassment to try to get you back. Think of whatever you can do to not be a target for the violence. For example, arrange for a safe place to stay. Arrange not to be alone at school, or on the way to and from school. *Include other people in your safety plan—your friends, your parents, sisters, brothers, neighbors, people at school.* If you have become isolated and alienated from your parents and other people in your life, remember that they can be helpful. You need support from adults for you to be safe.

Have someone else or a machine answer the telephone if you do not want to take your abuser's calls. If you are going out together, arrange to have a backup plan for getting home safely, and make sure someone knows where you are. Use what you know about your abuser's patterns and use all of your resources to come up with safety plans that will work for you.

• *Self-defense.* There are many ways to make it clear to your abuser you won't allow violence. Planning for your own safety is one important way. You can let your abuser know loudly and clearly that you won't be hit, or you won't have sex unless you want it. You can tell people about the abuser's violent behavior, rather than hiding it. You can take a self-defense class. Self-defense classes will teach you an attitude of strength and assertiveness, and how to deal with fear.

• *Use the legal system.* Assaults, beatings, sexual coercion, rape—these are illegal. Your abuser's violence against you is a crime.

You can complain to authorities such as the police, to your school administrators or security police, to your dorm advisor if you are away at college. Even if you are under eighteen, you can call the police. Violent boyfriends or girlfriends can be charged with:

Criminal harassment: subjecting you to physical contact, following you around or phoning you continually if it is done to harass, alarm or annoy you.

Reckless endangerment: placing you in serious fear of bodily injury or death.

Assault: intentionally or negligently causing or attempting to cause bodily injury.

Aggravated assault: intentionally or negligently causing or attempting to cause grave injury, as with a weapon.

Rape or attempted rape: sexual intercourse (penetration of the vagina) forced by violence or threat of violence.

Sexual assault: touching, rubbing, stroking or using objects in a sex act forced by violence or the threat of violence. Also, touching, rubbing or stroking by an adult of someone who is under eighteen.

Sodomy: forced penetration of the anus.

Forced oral sex.

You can get a *restraining order.* They are available to teens with help from an adult. A restraining order is an order by the court to the abuser to keep away from you. If the abuser violates the court order, he (or she) can be arrested. You file a request for a restraining order with a civil court. Call a nearby domestic violence hotline for information about how to get a restraining order in your area.

• *Tell an adult about the violence.* Tell an adult about your experiences with violence. Begin by telling your parents. You need support to solve this problem, because you cannot handle it alone. Talking to friends can help you feel supported and not so alone. They can help with your safety plan. But you must also talk to adults. Other adult family members you can talk to, besides your parents, may be good sources of support and help. At school, counselors, nurses, vice principals, principals or teachers can help. Sometimes a co-worker or a neighbor or a friend's parent can be helpful. *Find someone you can talk to.*

You may need to tell them more than once because they may not believe at first that you could be having such a serious problem. Or you might change your mind because when the violence stops for a while, you think it won't happen again. But keep telling them.

If you have been in an abusive relationship for a while, your relationship with your parent or parents may be very complicated by now. Your parents may want to help, but not know how, or they may not understand your strong fears and feelings. Or your parents may be angry with you, or they may not be supportive of you in general. The first step is to try to get their support by telling them exactly what has happened, and why you are afraid of your abuser. If you have been sexually or emotionally abused, this may be difficult to explain. Tell them about specific incidents. You may show them this book, and sections that apply to your experience.

If you see a counselor first, plan with the counselor how to tell your parents. If your parents do not listen or help, you might feel hurt and angry. You might even feel that you are better off not confronting your abuse. But you must keep trying, and find an adult who will listen.

• *Call a hotline for information.* Most cities have teen hotlines, domestic violence and rape hotlines, or crisis hotlines. There is a National Domestic Violence Hotline in the United States (1-800-333-7233). It does not cost money to call this hotline number. Hotlines can help teens who are abusers, or who are afraid they will be abusers, as well as teens who have been abused. They can help gay teens as well as straight teens. They can help friends and family members of someone who has a problem with dating violence.

You can find the phone number of local hotlines by looking in the telephone book under "teen" or "youth" or "rape" or "domestic violence" or "family violence" or "crisis." If you can't find it in the phone book, call information and tell the operator what you are looking for. The operator may know how it is listed.

Hotlines have trained counselors answering the phone. Some hotlines answer calls twenty-four hours a day, seven days a week. Others answer during certain hours, which you find out when you call. The hotline counselors can help you if you're upset and need someone to talk to. They can help if you have questions and need information. They can tell you how to find a counselor, or a legal service, or a support group near your home. They don't usually ask for your name, or they ask only for your first name, so you can feel safe that no one will know you or find out that you called.

• *Find a counselor or support group.* Talking to a counselor or therapist who knows about dating violence can help you sort out your confused feelings and become stronger in coping with the violence. Counseling can help you recover from the trauma you have experienced. A support group where you can talk with other girls or guys having the same or similar problems can help you so you don't feel so isolated and alone. You can learn from one another how to handle the problems that come up every day when you are in an abusive relationship, or when you have just ended one.

Your school counselor, your school nurse, a friend, a teen hotline or a domestic violence hotline in your area may be able to suggest places to go for counseling. If your school has a counseling center, you might be able to find a counselor at your school.

Advice from Abused Teens

"I would say once he hits you the first time, that is your chance to get out of the relationship. You should end it right there, because if you keep saying it's not going to happen again, you're going to keep repeatedly saying that. And pretty soon it's going to be too late."
—*Anonymous, 18*

"Leave him alone altogether. If it means changing your phone number or relocating, do it."—*Don, 18*

"I want my education, to get a job. I have to learn different things so I don't get stuck. If he does it again, I know I'm not going to stay again. Now I'm thinking about my future. Maybe you don't leave him because you're scared of the guy or of his friends. Maybe you have no way out, no money, nowhere else to go. The main thing is to go to school. Get training. Be strong,

talk to a friend or other people who have been abused."—Consuela, 19

"My advice to other girls is to tell the person who is hitting you or controlling you to stop it. Tell them, 'If you don't like something I do, tell me. Let me be myself.' I learned from being abused by my girlfriend, if you start hitting back, or hurting back, it gets worse. Don't let yourself get into that. If that person needs to go away, let her or him."—Meybel, 19

"I can look back on my relationship not with shame but with pride. I am proud of my own courage, which enabled me to grow strong. I am proud that I had the strength to say no to an abusive relationship. I can look back at my younger self and see in her the beginnings of a fighter, someone who would insist that she deserved something better than violence. I became someone who loves herself enough to settle for nothing less than happiness and self-respect."—Marge, 18

Advice for Abused Girls from Abusive Guys Who Have Changed

"Leave and find someone else. You don't need someone who's hitting you all the time."—Paul, 18

"I want to tell girls to get out of the relationship. Unless he becomes aware of the problem and wants to change, he won't change."—Ruiz, 17

"Call the police."—Barry, 18

"Keep away from him when he's going to rage at you. If he has to get out of the house or get away from you to cool off, let him go."—Leonard, 16

"I learned that a guy shouldn't want to have sex with a girl who doesn't want to. It isn't normal. If she's crying or begging him to stop or afraid of him, and he makes her do it anyway, that's sick. That is rape. I want to tell girls not to think that's normal."—Albert, 17

■ *What To Do if You Are Being Abused:*

- *Take it seriously*
- *Tell your abuser the violence must stop*
- *Say it clearly if you don't want sex*
- *Plan for your safety*
- *Tell your parents or a trusted adult*
- *Call the police or other authorities*
- *Call a hotline*
- *Find a counselor or a support group*
- *Talk to friends*
- *Do things for yourself that make you feel stronger*
- *Take a self-defense class*

Exercise

Use this blank page to write about your feelings or to make notes for yourself. Think about a plan of action for yourself.

12 *What Can You Do If You Are Abusive?*

"I was sure I'd never hit a girl because my dad beat my mom. But I felt I had to have control, and I did. I had a hard time trusting girls. I used to hit [my girlfriend], punch her, slap her. I told her she was no good and called her a slut. I choked her and threatened to kill her. Now I am working on my issues in counseling. I have learned to talk to [my girlfriend] and use a time out when I am angry. I now can look at what she is going through."—Paul, 18

"I emotionally abused her by telling her one thing and doing the opposite. I controlled her dress, behavior and who she could be friends with. I used my gang to intimidate her by pointing out victims and threatening to do the same to her. Now I think about negative consequences for assault like jail. I also think about how it affects her."—Ruiz, 17

If you have a problem with violent behavior, if you are emotionally or sexually abusive, you must find ways to change your behavior so that you don't hurt someone you care about. In the long run, you are hurting yourself.

You *can* control your anger so that you don't hurt anyone. No matter what anyone else does, you have the choice to act in a way that is not violent. You have the choice to act with self-respect and respect for others.

It is illegal to harass or assault someone, including someone you are in a relationship with. There are serious consequences for harassing, assaulting or sexually assaulting someone. You can be kicked out of school. You can be arrested. You can go to jail.

You CAN Stop the Violence

How can you keep yourself from being violent?

• *Acknowledge that you have a problem.* The first step in overcoming a problem with violence is to say to yourself and to others, "I have a problem. I don't want to be abusive." If you feel that you want to control your violence so that your girlfriend won't leave you, then that is a beginning.

But you have to want it for yourself, whether your girlfriend leaves or stays. It is hard to change. It takes a lot of courage. You need a vision of yourself in the future: calm, secure, able to control yourself, accepting of yourself and not blaming others for your problems. You need a sense deep inside you that you know you can be different, and that you can make your life better.

Make a commitment to yourself: I will not hit. I will not force or coerce sex. I will not emotionally attack or manipulate.

• *Find a counselor or support group.* Counseling can help you understand your problems and your feelings. Counseling can help you learn ways to handle your anger without hurting anyone. You can learn about your cycle of violence and recognize your own behavior patterns. Then you can find ways to stop yourself before you lose control. You can learn empathy for your girlfriend or boyfriend, to understand how she or he feels when you treat her or him badly. You can learn about healthy sex and love.

Counseling can help you find out about your feelings and why you react the way that you do.

If you join a group with others who have the same problem, you can learn how others deal with relationships. You can get support from other guys to find new ways to act with girls, and new ways to cope with frustration, stress and anger.

• *Join Alcoholics Anonymous or a drug program.* If you are abusing drugs or alcohol, then you are not dealing with your problem with violence. If your excuse for being violent is that you were drunk, then you have to stop drinking and deal directly with your violence. Take responsibility for it. When you are sober or clean, you can seriously say to yourself, I have a problem to solve. And you can start the process of solving your problems rather than escaping from them.

• *Educate yourself.* Read about relationship violence, about people who have overcome it, about how it affects its victims. Talk to others about it. Watch television shows and movies about it. Learn as much as you can to understand your experiences.

Confronting your violence means changing your attitudes towards women in general, and towards victims, and developing respect for them. It means changing your attitudes about violence, until you believe that it is not acceptable.

Advice from Abusive Guys Who Have Changed

"Try and get help. Join violent offender groups. Stop and think before something happens that could ruin your or someone else's life. Don't deny emotions." —*Allen, 18*

"A 'real man' respects and pleases a girl during sex. A 'real man' doesn't want to force or trick a girl to do it.

Think about it—are you a 'real man'?"—Barry, 18

"Look at what you're doing to your girlfriend and put yourself in her shoes. How would you like it?"
—Paul, 18

"Nobody controls you. You can control yourself. You make your own choices. It's not okay to retaliate."
—Ray, 18

"Think of the consequences."—David, 17

"It's a cycle beginning with verbal abuse and turns into physical abuse against people you care for."—Steve, 20

"Walk away before things get heated up. If you can't do that, you should get help. It's not right to hit girls."
—Gilbert, 17

■ What To Do if You Are an Abuser:

- *Say to yourself, "I have a problem. I am abusive."*
- *Make a commitment to yourself: "I will NOT rape or hit."*
- *Call a hotline*
- *Find a counselor or support group*
- *Talk to parents, friends, other adults about your problem*
- *Learn as much as you can about abusive relationships*
- *Go to Alcoholics Anonymous or a drug program*
- *Respect women*
- *Respect yourself: You CAN choose not to abuse*

Exercise

Use this blank page to write about your feelings or to make notes for yourself. Think about a plan of action for yourself to deal with this problem.

13 What Can You Do If Your Friend Is in an Abusive Relationship?

"I was there and he got real mad. First he started screaming at her and calling her names. Then he shoved her into the car and started slapping her. She was scared and tried to tell him that she loved him. I got mad and yelled at him to stop, that she didn't do anything wrong. My boyfriend also tried to get him to stop. He put his hand on his arm and told him to calm down, that this was no way to treat a girlfriend. Later, we talked with her, and kept telling her he had no right to hit her."
—Mercedes, 19

"At first I tried to tell him to leave but he didn't want to hear about it. I didn't know what to do. So I was just there for him."—Roy, 18

"My friend came running over to help me. If it hadn't been for her, I might be dead. He kept trying to smother me. . . . My friend got me to the school—and said that if I didn't press charges, she would."—Salina, 13

If you have a friend who is being victimized in an abusive relationship, what can you do?

• **Help your friend recognize the abuse.** Ask questions and talk about what is happening to her or him. Help your friend to see that what is happening is not normal and to see the signs of abuse. Tell her or him that it will probably get worse.

• *Support your friend's strength.* Recognize the things that your friend does to take care of her or himself. Encourage your friend's strengths and courage. Encourage your friend to do things with you, and with other friends, to have some enjoyment apart from the relationship.

• *Be non-judgmental.* Try to see that your friend is confused because she or he is frightened by the violence, but wants the love or security from being with the boyfriend or girlfriend. If your friend wants to stay in the relationship, or goes back and forth about it, try not to tell her or him that she or he is wrong. Tell her or him that you are worried about her or his safety and self-respect. Help your friend see that she or he is not to blame for the violence. Help your friend recognize the abuser's excuses for being violent (which blame the victim).

• *Help your friend with safety plans.* Help your friend focus on being safe. Help her or him use what she or he knows about particular resources and about the abuser's patterns to figure out ways to be safe when the abuser is explosive or violent, or verbally or sexually abusive. For example, if your friend is a girl who is being abused or harassed by her boyfriend, walk with her to school or have her stay over at your house when he is threatening her.

• *Be there. Listen.* Even if your friend breaks up with the abuser and goes back, listen. Support her or his strength. Eventually your friend will leave, especially with the support of friends.

• *If your friend breaks up with the abuser, keep up the support.* It takes a while to get over a relationship that is violent. Keep in close contact through the times she or he feels lonely, or scared, or bad about her or himself. Your friend may feel like getting back together. She or he may miss the boyfriend or girlfriend, or may not feel strong enough to re-sist the pressure to get back together.

• *Help your friend talk to adults to get help.* Talk with your friend about telling parents or other adults. Go with her or him to see a counselor or to enroll in a support group. If she or he won't talk to an adult, then *you must find an adult you trust to talk to* about it. Ask your parents or a school counselor, nurse or administrator. Ask the adult to help, to reach out, to intervene. Talk to your friend's par-ents about what is happening to your friend. Don't assume that your friend's parents know about the abuse.

• *If you become frightened or frustrated, get support from friends and family members or other adults.* Educate yourself about dating violence. *You can't rescue your friend.* You can't neglect your own life to take care of her or him. But with support for yourself, you can calmly hang in there and support your friend as she or he goes through the ups and downs of dealing with the violence in her or his life.

14 You Can Have a Healthy Relationship

"After breaking up with Andy, . . . I [gradually] became more relaxed, and I wasn't afraid to say what I wanted to anyone anymore. [My new boyfriend] holds me when I get upset and lets me cry. Never does he put me down or even come close to hitting me. We can argue. He is so patient."—Anonymous, 14

In healthy relationships, young men and women make decisions thoughtfully together and communicate with each other. When they disagree, they argue and discuss their differences. They listen to each other's viewpoints and feelings. When they have a conflict, they negotiate. They find a way to compromise so that they can both get what they need. When one of them gets angry or loses their temper, they calm themselves down so they won't hurt themselves or anyone else. For example, Linda said:

"I got so upset when John insisted that I come over to his house for Christmas. We were so mad at each other. I wanted to be with him, but I wanted to be with my family. We talked and finally worked it out together. We spent Christmas Eve with my family and Christmas Day with his."

If one feels hurt by the other, they can talk about it. They can apologize without feeling humiliated or afraid. If one feels like having time alone, or wants to do things separately, their boyfriend or girlfriend can accept it. Thomas said:

> *"Right after school, or sometimes when I lose my temper, I just want to watch TV by myself, you know, to chill out. On the days when I go home from school with Judy, I have to explain, 'I'll see ya later.' Usually she wants to hang out with me right after school, but she gets it. I'll be better to hang out with later. We don't get jealous or anything like that."*

If either one of them approaches the other to have sex and the other one doesn't want to, they talk about it, and stop. Or they talk about it and change what they were doing so that both of them are comfortable. Both feel free to stop at any time during sex. Josh said:

> *"When my girlfriend started crying and said she just couldn't go down on me, I held her and said we didn't have to unless she wanted to."*

They trust that the other will understand. They are careful to discuss how to protect themselves from AIDS and pregnancy. They feel respected and cared for.

They have fun together and they are free to enjoy themselves. They are not afraid that they will be cruelly hurt if they say or do something that their boyfriend or girlfriend thinks is wrong. Valerie said:

> *"I didn't know what to do. I knew I'd be late, but I couldn't reach Lisa to tell her. I thought she'd be so mad, and I was scared because of how my last girlfriend used to attack me over every little thing. Lisa was mad, and worried, and she told me how mad she was. But she also listened and believed me when I explained what happened. It was over in a minute!"*

There is no room for fear in a healthy relationship. Each person trusts the other. They can enjoy each other's successes at school, in sports or other activities. They can enjoy that their girlfriend or boyfriend has lots of friends and interests and dreams for the future. Trudy said:

"I told my boyfriend, James, about this guy in my class who works at this place where I just got a job. The guy told me all about the place, so now I'm not so nervous. James said I was lucky to know someone already."

They would not try to restrict or control one another. They would not keep their girlfriend or boyfriend from doing things because of their own fears. They encourage and support one another. Selma said:

"You know what I like best about Tony? He's on my team. It's going to be hard to get through all the years of college I have ahead of me. He cheers me on every step of the way! We do that for each other."

Exercise

Use this blank page to write about your feelings or to make notes for yourself. Write about what it would be like to be in a healthy relationship.

Footnotes

1   D. Sugarman and G. Hotaling (1991). Dating Violence: A Review of Contextual and Risk Factors. In B. Levy, ed., *Dating Violence: Young Women in Danger*. Seattle: Seal Press.

2   S. Ageton (1983). *Sexual Assault Among Adolescents*. Lexington, MA: Heath.

3   E. Kessner (1988). Sweetheart Murders: When Teen Boyfriends Turn into Killers. *Redbook*, March, 130–189.

4   J. Toth, New Study of Domestic Violence Finds Mandatory Arrests Backfire. *Los Angeles Times*, December 18, 1991, A5.

5   D. Sugarman and G. Hotaling, ibid.

6   J. Henton, R. Cate, J. Koval, S. Lloyd, and S. Christopher (1983). Romance and Violence in Dating Relationships. *Journal of Family Issues*, 4, 467–482.

7   D. Sugarman and G. Hotaling, ibid.

Resources

Suggested Reading

Bateman, Py. *Macho: Is That Really What You Want?* Seattle: Alternatives to Fear, 1986. Helps boys fight negative peer pressure and learn new ways to relate to girls.

Chaiet, Donna. *Staying Safe on Dates.* New York: Rosen Publishing Group, 1995. Uses real-life situations to illustrate how to handle various dating situations, including how to set verbal and emotional boundaries for a relationship and how to deal with sexual assault and rape.

Hicks, John. *Dating Violence: True Stories of Hurt and Hope.* Brookfield, Conn: Millbrook Press, 1996. Discusses the characteristics and dangers of unhealthy relationships, the importance of honest communication and cooperative ways of resolving conflicts.

Jones, Ann, and Susan Schechter. *When Love Goes Wrong: What to do When You Can't Do Anything Right.* New York: HarperCollins, 1993. Provides guidance and practical options for women in controlling and abusive relationships.

McShane, Claudette. *Warning! Dating may be hazardous to your health.* Racine, Wis: Mother Courage Press, 1988. Using first-person accounts, explains the issue of dating violence, why it happens, the healing process and prevention. Aimed at women of all ages.

Miklowitz, Gloria. *Past Forgiving.* New York: Simon and Shuster Books for Young Readers, 1995. Fifteen-year-old Alexandra finds that her boyfriend Cliff demands all her time, isolates her by his jealousy and eventually becomes physically abusive.

Rue, Nancy. *Coping with Dating Violence.* New York: Rosen Publishing Group, 1989. Examines the characteristics of abusive relationships and gives advice on how to avoid or get out of such relationships.

Rue, Nancy, and Rudolf Steiner. *Everything You Need to Know About Abusive Relationships*. New York: Rosen Publishing Group, 1996. Discusses different kinds of abuse that occurs between teens who are dating and offers advice on how to handle abusive situations.

Warshaw, Robin. *I Never Called it Rape: The Ms. Report on Recognizing, Fighting, and Surviving Date and Acquaintance Rape*. New York: Harper and Row, 1988. Discusses the *Ms.* Magazine Campus Project on Sexual Assault. Includes many statistics, clear definitions and first-hand accounts.

Videos

Breaking the Chain: Building Healthy Relationships. Twenty-three minute video about a young man with an abusive father who is in danger of becoming abusive himself. He seeks counseling in order to learn anger management and communication skills. 1992. The Bureau for At-Risk Youth, 135 Dupont Street, P.O. Box 760, Plainview, NY 11803-0760.

In Love and In Danger. Fifteen-minute documentary video designed to educate parents, teachers and teens about the dynamics of relationship violence. Developed by The Junior League of Ann Arbor and produced by Victor/Harder Productions. Distributed by Intermedia, 800-553-8336, and Sunburst Communications, 800-431-1934.

Rough Love. Fifty-minute program that creates a dialogue between teens, families, friends and professionals about the dynamics and consequences of teen dating violence. 1996. National Coalition Against Domestic Violence, P.O. Box 18749, Denver, CO 80218.

Organizations and Hotlines

Battered Women's Alternative
Hotline: 888-215-5555
P.O. Box 6406
Concord, CA 94524
510-676-2845
Offers counseling, support groups and local referrals. Can provide classroom presentations, peer advocacy and peer counseling.

Child Help USA
Hotline: 800-422-4453
www.childhelp.com
Offers crisis intervention and local referrals.

Covenant House
Hotline: 800-999-9999
460 West 41st Street
New York, NY 10011
Provides international crisis intervention. Caller can request printed materials on dating violence.

Gay and Lesbian Anti-Violence Project
Hotline: 212-807-0197
647 Hudson Street
New York, NY 10014
Provides advocacy in the New York area for Gay, Lesbian, Bisexual and Transgendered people.

March of Dimes Birth Defects
755 Sansome Street, 2nd Floor
San Francisco, CA 94111
415-788-2202
Provides information on battering during teen pregnancy. The Prevention of Battering During Teen Pregnancy project will be featured on a weekly Internet chat-line for teens called *The In-Site,* www.theinsite.com.

National Coalition Against Domestic Violence
P.O. Box 18749
Denver, CO 80218-0749
303-839-1852
www.webmerchants.com/ncadv
Provides crisis intervention and local referrals. Offers a video with teacher's guide, *Rough Love,* and a book entitled *Teen Dating Violence Resource Manual.* Call for a catalog.

National Council on Child Abuse and Family Violence
Hotline: 800-222-2000
1155 Connecticut Ave NW, Suite 400
Washington, DC 20036
202-429-6695

Can refer callers to other hot lines, and can mail three information sheets: "Teenage Power, Control, and Will," "Teen Dating Violence Reading List" and "Danger Ahead: Early Warning Signs of Teen Dating Violence."

National Domestic Violence Hotline: 800-799-7233

Teen Moms Shelter
Hotline: 800-693-2247
Only serves teens in the Bay Area but can provide information, support, counseling and referrals to teens throughout the nation.

Youth Crisis
Hotline: 800-448-4663
P.O. Box 178408
San Diego, CA 92177-8408
619-292-5683
www.ydi.org
email: ydi@ydi.org
Provides intervention in crisis situations.

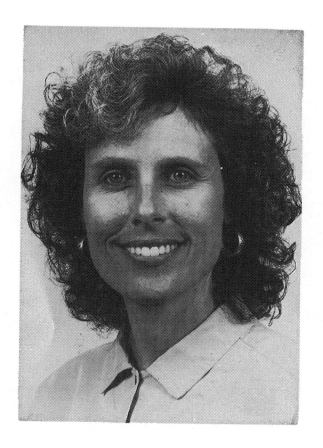

Barrie Levy, M.S.W., is the editor of *Dating Violence: Young Women in Danger,* and the co-author of *What Parents Need to Know About Dating Violence* and *50 Ways to a Safer World: Everyday Actions You Can Take to Prevent Violence in Neighborhoods, Schools and Communities.* Active in the movement to prevent violence against women for 25 years, she is a psychotherapist, consultant and trainer, and is on the faculty of the Departments of Social Welfare and Women's Studies at the University of California, Los Angeles.

Selected New Leaf Titles from Seal Press

Getting Free: You Can End Abuse and Take Back Your Life, 15th anniversary edition, by Ginny NiCarthy. $12.95, 1-878067-92-3. Also Available on Audiocassette: 60 minutes, $10.95, 0-931188-84-9.

You Can Be Free: An Easy-to-Read Handbook for Abused Women by Ginny NiCarthy and Sue Davidson. $8.95, 0-878067-06-0.

New Beginnings: A Creative Writing Guide for Women Who Have Left Abusive Partners by Sharon Doane, M.S.W. $10.95, 1-878067-78-8.

Dating Violence: Young Women in Danger, edited by Barrie Levy. $18.95. 1-58005-001-8.

Naming the Violence: Speaking Out Against Lesbian Battering, edited by Kerry Lobel. $12.95, 0-931188-42-3.

Mejor Sola Que Mal Acompañada: For the Latina in an Abusive Relationship/Para la Mujer Golpeada by Myrna M. Zambrano. $12.95, 0-931188-26-1.

Chain Chain Change: For Black Women in Abusive Relationships, expanded second edition, by Evelyn C. White. $8.95, 1-878067-60-5.

Mommy and Daddy Are Fighting: A Book for Children About Family Violence by Susan Paris. $8.95, 0-931188-33-4.

A Community Secret: For the Filipina in an Abusive Relationship by Jacqueline Agtuca, in collaboration with The Asian Women's Shelter. $5.95, 1-878067-44-3.

The Ones Who Got Away: Women Who Left Abusive Partners by Ginny NiCarthy. $12.95, 0-931188-49-0.

Called to Account by M'Liss Switzer and Katherine Hale. $8.95, 0-931188-55-5.

Talking It Out: A Guide to Groups for Abused Women by Ginny NiCarthy, Karen Merriam and Sandra Coffman. $12.95, 0-931188-24-5.

Ordering Information

Individuals: You can order directly from us by calling our toll-free number, 1-800-754-0271.

Non-profit Organizations and Women's Shelters: Please call customer service at the number above for information about our quantity discounts.

Seal Press
3131 Western Avenue, Suite 410
Seattle, Washington 98121
Phone (206) 283-7844
Fax (206) 285-9410
Email: sealprss@scn.org
Visit our website at www.sealpress.com